GROWING OLDER IN GOD'S GRACE

Larry Swaim, Th.D.

ISBN: 978-0-89098-893-0

©2018, 2023 by 21st Century Christian, Inc
Nashville, TN 37215
All rights reserved.

All rights reserved. No part of this publication may be reproduced, stored in a retrieval system, or transmitted in any form or by any means—electronic, mechanical, photocopy, recording, digital, or otherwise—without the written permission of the publisher.

Unless otherwise noted Scripture quotations are from the English Standard Version. Scripture quotations are from The Holy Bible, English Standard Version® (ESV®), copyright © 2001 by Crossway, a publishing ministry of Good News Publishers.
Used by permission. All rights reserved.

Unless otherwise noted Scripture quotations are from the New International Version. Scripture quotations taken from
THE HOLY BIBLE, NEW INTERNATIONAL VERSION®, NIV®
Copyright © 1973, 1978, 1984, 2011 by Biblica, Inc.™
Used by permission. All rights reserved worldwide.

Unless otherwise noted Scripture quotations are from the New King James Version. Scripture taken from the New King James Version.
Copyright © 1982 by Thomas Nelson, Inc. Used by permission. All rights reserved.

Cover design by Jonathan Edelhuber

ACKNOWLEDGMENTS

Many thanks to Cathy Brown, my transcriber, editor, and proofreader without whose assistance, the writing of this book would not have been possible.

DEDICATIONS

Dedicated to my wife, LaDonna;
and my children:
Cynthia, Lance, and Suzanne;
my grandchildren:
Taylor, Hayley, Kelsey, Megan, and Katherine;
and my great-grandchildren:
Lila, Lincoln, and Cohen.

TABLE OF CONTENTS

Introduction 7

CHAPTER 1
A Senior Citizen in Christ's Church............................ 9

CHAPTER 2
The Soul 21

CHAPTER 3
Maturity... 31

CHAPTER 4
Forgetting the Past 45

CHAPTER 5
We Need One Another: Fellowship........................... 55

CHAPTER 6
Worry – Anxiety 65

CHAPTER 7
Becoming An Encourager 79

CHAPTER 8
Adjusting to Change.. 91

CHAPTER 9
Live as Positively as Possible 105

CHAPTER 10
The Privilege of Being a Grandparent...................... 113

CHAPTER 11
The Importance of Love 123

CHAPTER 12
Preparing to Die.. 131

CHAPTER 13
Going Home – Heaven 141

Bibliography 149

INTRODUCTION

Growing older is a privilege not everyone can enjoy. For those who do reach their senior years, however, it is a period of time filled with both opportunity and significant challenges. Each period of our lives has its own unique opportunities, and our senior years are no exception. We have the incredible opportunity of influencing grandchildren—sometimes even great grandchildren—and of being an example of true Christian longevity to those younger members of our congregation. It is a time during which we may be tempted to retire completely from Christianity and turn the work of the church over entirely to the younger members, which is understandable to some. It is also true, however, that the younger members of the congregation need the wisdom and experience of older Christians. There should be a true, mutual respect between the older and younger members of the Lord's church.

In this book we will discuss many of the opportunities and challenges of older age. The subject matter is meant to inspire discussion when the book is used as a classroom reference. As we grow older, each of us has our own experiences and stories to tell and the opportunity to be inspired by those older biblical characters who successfully traversed the often difficult path of growing older. It is my sincere prayer that this book will be challenging, uplifting, and hopefully even inspiring, and that each chapter as it is read and studied will bring us a clear realization of the wonderful and unique privileges that we have as older Christians in God's kingdom.

CHAPTER 1

A SENIOR CITIZEN IN CHRIST'S CHURCH

Introduction

After birth, we begin to progress through different ages, stages, passages, and transitions. We move from infancy, to toddlerhood, to childhood, to adolescence, to teen years, to young adult, to middle age, and finally to the beginning of the golden years. People enter and leave these various stages at different ages in their lives, so I have developed a litmus test to see if you are qualified to be called a senior citizen.

1. Do you ever feel confused?
2. Do you feel frustrated and overwhelmed?
3. Are you a little more forgetful than in the past?
4. Are you experiencing more fatigue?
5. Is an afternoon nap more appealing?
6. Are you spending more time at doctors' offices or in the hospital?
7. Do you have more aches and pains than in the past?
8. Are you less patient with your spouse, other family members, or friends?
9. Are you taking more medications?
10. Do you feel unappreciated, alone, misunderstood, even angry, for no apparent reason?
11. Do you lose things more often?
12. Are little problems becoming big problems?
13. Are you less active?

14. Do you gain weight more easily and lose it slower?
15. Have you had body parts replaced—hips, knees, valves, stents, etc.?
16. Do you have a major illness, which has become all-consuming in your life?
17. Are you always in pain?
18. Does change bother you?
19. Is your hearing or sight growing worse?
20. Does heaven mean more to you now than it previously did?

If you answered even one half of these questions with a yes, it is a good indication you are a senior citizen.

Retirement Is Called Heaven

Ever since Adam and Eve, older people have experienced similar problems in the aging process. If we live long enough, we will not only experience, but suffer through, the physical, mental, and sometimes spiritual problems associated with aging. In order to successfully travel the dangerous path of aging, we must develop a sense of humor. This will allow us to avoid the bitterness and cynicism that often come with aging. We must learn to laugh at ourselves, to be humble, and able to see the humor in many of the limitations and disabilities of growing old. For this reason, I will begin each chapter with a little humor or wisdom. I wish I could remember where I have found all of the humorous stories and examples that I will be using. Unfortunately, over the years I have simply clipped out and put in file folders humorous stories, often losing the source. I will give the source when available.

A Little Humor

Have you noticed the stairs are getting steeper, groceries are getting heavier, and everything is further away than it used to be? Yesterday I walked to the corner and I was dumbfounded to discover just how long our street has become. And you know people are less considerate now, especially the younger ones. They speak in whispers all the time. If you ask them to speak up they just keep repeating themselves, endlessly mouthing the same silent message until they are red in the face. What do they think I am—a lip reader? I also think they are much younger than I was at the same age. On the other hand, people my own age are much older than I am. [My mother at 96 in the independent living home kept referring to all of the people around her, most younger than her, as "those old people."] I ran into an old friend the other day, and she didn't even recognize me! I got to thinking about the poor dear while I was combing my hair this morning and in doing so, I glanced at my own reflection. Well, goodness gracious! Really, now even mirrors are not made the way they used to be. Another thing. Everyone drives so fast these days. You are risking life and limb if you happen to pull onto the freeway in front of them.

All I can say is, their brakes must wear out awfully fast, the way I see them screeching and swerving in my rear view mirror.

Clothing manufacturers are less civilized these day too. Why else would they suddenly start labeling a size 10 or 12 dress as an 18 or 20? Do they think nobody notices what they do? The people who make bathroom scales are pulling the same prank. Do they think I actually believe the number I see on that dial? Ha! I would never let myself weigh that much. Just who do these people think they are fooling? (USWU, *"Age Is Only a Number"*)

We Are Living Longer

With our incredible medical advancements and by eating well and exercising regularly, people are living longer and healthier than ever. Yet, when we reach a certain age, we are expected to automatically begin to think and behave as an older person. Retirement ages are often dictated to us by government, business, and family expectations. *Retirement* is a word I have tried to eliminate from my vocabulary, because in most important ways, we should never retire. We may experience changes in emphasis of our work and how we spend our time, but we should never get to the point where our goal is simply to do nothing but play, nap, and watch TV. That is the essence of a second childhood.

Bible Examples
- Joshua was old when he began leading the children of Israel into the Promised Land. At 85 he delivered a powerful speech, speaking of the strength he had received from the Lord.
- Moses was 80 years old when he led the people toward the Promised Land.
- Abraham was 75 years old when he left Terah to start a new life in a strange, distant land, and he was 100 years old when he fathered Isaac.
- Sarah was 90 years old when she bore Isaac.
- Daniel served under four kings and had great influence throughout his entire life.
- In his old age, Noah was still pounding pegs and finishing the ark, defying skepticism and criticism, remaining faithful to God's words, even in the face of the harshest rejection.
- Job, as he approached old age, had to start all over again. He had lost everything important to him in the first part of his life, but regained it, along with even more in the latter part of his life. It was all because of his faithfulness and trust in God.
- Joseph, after having reached a mature age, came to the greatest test of his life: the test of forgiving those who had sinned against him. With grace and forgiveness, he proved that these two essential biblical qualities will carry us far in life.
- David lived a very long life. At the end of his life, he suffered greatly. Part of that suffering may have been as a result of the sins of his earlier life. We do reap what we sow. But part of it was simply the aging process. He obviously had poor circulation, and Abishag, the Shunammite woman became the first

human bed warmer, keeping David warm and comfortable in a non-sexual way.
- Saul, however, as he approached old age, allowed bitterness, jealousy, and resentment to be the predominant qualities of his life, overshadowing an otherwise acceptable life when he was younger. Bitterness, anger, and jealousy do more harm to the container in which they are stored than to anyone on whom they are poured. These qualities destroy us from the inside out. They may steal away previous victories.
- Solomon, during a portion of his later years, was quite discontented, having experienced all of the pleasures and material benefits this life can afford. But he finally experienced a revitalization of spirit when he began to recognize what the real priorities of this existence should be; that is, to acknowledge God, serving Him and others. Solomon said, "The end of the matter; all has been heard. Fear God and keep his commandments, for this is the whole duty of man" (Ecclesiastes 12:13).
- Isaiah and Jeremiah, great prophets of God, continued to speak their words of history and prophecy until the end of their lives.
- Paul referred to himself as an "old man" (Philemon 1:9), but as an old man he continued to work in the kingdom of God. The psalmist said, "My mouth is filled with your praise, and with your glory all the day. Do not cast me off in the time of old age; forsake me not when my strength is spent" (Psalm 71:8, 9).
- Peter lived to be an old man and continued working all of his life, serving as an elder in the Jerusalem church.
- John wrote the book of Revelation as an aged man on the isle of Patmos.
- Zachariah and Elizabeth were past their childbearing years, yet God visited them and instructed them they would have a son. This wonderful couple, who believed the voice of God and were true to His word, became the parents of John the Baptist.

CHAPTER 1

Let's examine the life of Anna. The daughter of Phanuel, Anna was married only seven years when she was widowed. She remained a widow for at least 84 years. Luke 2:37, 38 says, "She did not depart from the temple, worshiping with fasting and prayer night and day. And coming up at that very hour she began to give thanks to God and to speak of him to all who were waiting for the redemption of Jerusalem." When we look at this great woman's life—a woman who was either 91 or 105, depending on how you calculate the time—she was in every way a model older person. During her life, she no doubt experienced much loss and sorrow, yet she did not allow it to make her bitter or resentful. Rather, she kept herself busy in God's work and spent much of her time in fasting and prayer. How wonderful it is to see an older person who has a lifetime of obedience and love for the Lord, one who has remained faithful through the good and bad times! She was rewarded by identifying the child Jesus.

Anna stayed busy. Her goal was to serve God and help others, remaining faithful to the first and second commandments. She did not isolate herself, although she did confine herself to the temple and to the work there, but she was also busy interacting with God's people as they came in and out to worship. Almost all of us who reach our senior years will have experienced much grief and trauma, as well as many losses that have brought tears to our eyes and hurt to our hearts. We cannot, however, allow these to cause us to pull our world in on top of us and not trust people or God or refuse to commit to good works and new relationships. We cannot live like turtles in a shell. We must have interaction with others, and the best interaction is with God's people. Anna kept busy doing God's work, interacting with and serving others. There is no doubt that Anna was a woman of God's Word, a prophetess who worshiped Him daily. In my life I have known several faithful, godly women who devoted themselves to studying God's Word, teaching it to younger women and children, exemplifying Christ in every way in their lives, and using all of their talents and abilities in God's service to others. What a wonderful legacy!

Anna also prayed regularly. Her prayers were heard. Her prayers sustained and uplifted her, giving her the strength and courage to continue in her service to God and others. Another wonderful quality of Anna's is that, at the end of her life, she never lost hope. There are so many older (and, I might add, some younger) who need a *hope transplant*. Difficult times, losses, pain and suffering, have taken away hope from so many. The aloneness of old age can cause one to lose hope. But Anna believed in the future, and she believed that she was to be an active, faithful part of that future. As we grow older, we must never lose hope. Hope is what sustains us in desperate times. Anna's faithfulness was rewarded by being able to hold and bless the infant Jesus.

All of these great men and women who lived beyond the middle age period of their lives were particularly distinguished by how they used their last years. Trust in God and His Word, attitude of mind, spirit, and character; all play an important part in how we deal with and successfully traverse growing older.

The History of Retirement

In the early history of man, there was no retirement. People worked and labored until death. In early biblical times, when there were a number of people who lived to very old age, retirement was not a part of their lifestyle. It was the culture that people continued to do whatever they could until they died. As history passed, the elderly population began to increase, and the numbers reached critical mass. "It was no longer just a matter of respecting the aged. Older people were everywhere, giving advice, repeating themselves, complaining about their health problems, trying to help, and often getting in the way of younger people in their quest for upward mobility."

CHAPTER 1

In 1883, Chancellor Otto von Bismarck of Germany had a problem. The Marxists were threatening to take control of Europe, so to help his countrymen resist that takeover, Bismarck announced that he would pay a pension to any non-working German over the age of 65. Bismarck was smart, because few people lived to be 65 at that time. Bismarck set an arbitrary world standard for future generations for the exact year at which old age would begin and established the precedent that government should pay people for growing old.

William Osler led the foundation for the scientific information regarding old age and retirement. In 1905 he delivered a valedictory address at Johns Hopkins Hospital where he had been a physician-in-chief. Osler said that it was a matter of fact that the years between 25 and 40 in a worker's career are the 15 golden years. He called that span the "constructive period." He went on to say that workers between the ages of 40 and 60 were mostly uncreative and therefore only tolerable. But after 60, the average worker was useless and should be put out to pasture.

Living Longer

Life Expectancy in the United States

   1600–44 years
   1700–47 years
   1800–60 years
   1900–71 years
   2016–79 years

We are an aging society.

In the U.S., a large number of aging factory workers were slowing down the assembly lines, taking too many personal days, and usurping the place of the younger, more productive men with families to support, causing increased unemployment among the young workers. These attitudes further reinforced the concept of retirement. During the Great Depression, when good jobs were hard to come by, the situation was intensified. Francis Townsend initiated a popular movement in California, proposing retirement at age 60. In exchange, the government would pay a pension of up to $200 a month. President Franklin D. Roosevelt felt this was too generous. And so, in 1935, he initiated the Social Security Act, which made workers pay for their old age insurance in advance. Thus began the current definition of retirement, which is "leaving your job between the ages of 62 and 65 and doing whatever you can afford to do to occupy your time." Then and now, most retired people wish there was something they could constructively do. Many have opted to volunteer their time to charitable organizations or to become entrepreneurs and begin second careers, but few relish the idea of retiring to a rocking chair, watching TV, or playing with their computer or phone all day.

Unions certainly have played their part in the retirement controversy, insisting on rigid guidelines for retirement and proposing even earlier retirement than 60 or 65 in situations in which they want a younger workforce to take over. There are certain occupations for which retirement comes even earlier. In the military, retirement age comes after 20 years of service. This is also the case with most first responder jobs such as fire, police, and emergency services, meaning that many in America retire from their first job around 40 years old. Then they are faced with the decision of beginning a new career or simply sitting back and waiting for true old age and death to overtake them.

What a Waste
There are 10,000 people in the U.S. reaching age 65 every day, many who have already retired or are in the process of retiring. The number is almost staggering: 10,000 new retirees every day. One of the greatest wastes of valuable resources is the disregarding

CHAPTER 1

of the experience, knowledge, influence, and maturity of these retirees who are put out to pasture and often disregarded and forgotten. Among these people are highly educated, informed, hard-working, healthy, mentally sharp individuals who still have so much to contribute to society, but are encouraged on every front to simply retire, get out of the way, enjoy yourself for the rest of your life, and become silent non-contributors.

I do not believe we are going to reverse the concept of retirement any time soon, but we certainly need to re-think the idea that those who are retiring no longer have a place in active society, business, politics, or religion. So many people are resisting the pressure for early retirement and view their last years as their best and most productive years in many areas. Some of the greatest accomplishments in the history of the world have come about because of people who refused to let an arbitrary age keep them from thinking, working, and being active in their particular field of expertise.

Grow old along with me! The best is yet to be,
The last of life, for which the first was made:
Our times are in His hand
Who saith, "A whole I planned, Youth shows but half;
trust God: see all, nor be afraid!"
by Robert Browning

Good Secular Examples

Winston Churchill was 77 when he entered his second term as prime minister of Great Britain. He served until he was 81, but he remained politically active until he was 91. Benjamin Franklin was 75 when he negotiated peace with Great Britain. He was 81 when he worked out the compromise that resulted in the U.S. Constitution. Michelangelo was 71 when he was appointed chief architect of St. Peter's Cathedral in Rome. He died at 89, still creating the beautiful frescos on the walls of the Pauline Chapel. You may not know the name, but Marion Rice Hart completed a solo trans-Atlantic flight in a single engine Beechcraft Bonanza when she was 84 years old. Frank Lloyd Wright, the great architect, was 91 years old when he completed New York's Guggenheim Museum. Yitzhak Shamir became prime minister of Israel when he was 76. At 84, he was still active in government, negotiating peace talks. Colonel Sanders was 65 when he established his first Colonel Sanders's Southern Fried Chicken business, which eventually became KFC. Mother Teresa was ministering in Calcutta and traveling around the world with her message of hope, peace, and love until she died at age 87. There are so many other people who accomplished great things in their older age, such as Albert Schweitzer, Florence Nightingale, and Billy Graham, who continued writing and inspiring into their nineties. We should never allow a number age to keep us from good work and accomplishments (Source: David Turner, *Biblical Studies*).

Often, when we age, we become uninvolved. Never lose your value. Engage with your children, your grandchildren, your friends, church, or wherever you find yourself. Each relationship adds value to your life. Our children, grandchildren, and great-grandchildren need to know our history. They need to know how we grew up, the circumstances and conditions of our youth. They need to know what we hold as valuable and important. They need to know we are patriotic, that we thank servicemen and women every time we see them, that we appreciate teachers, preachers, doctors, police, and others who devote themselves to helping us. One of our major responsibilities as a parent or grandparent is to educate our children and grandchildren on our values and history.

Retirement is not a biblical word, nor is it a biblical requirement. We can never retire from God's work or from our responsibilities to God. The Bible does speak eloquently about retirement. It's called heaven. Each of us has talents, abilities, and opportunities, and God has blessed each of us with certain unique resources. We need to use these in the kingdom of God and to His glory until death. That does not mean that as we get older we cannot refocus our attention and efforts. In fact, retiring from work can often open up new avenues of service to God. It is wrong to waste years of education, training, and skill development simply because the calendar turns to a certain date and age. We must be faithful till death.

Questions

1. Discuss some symptoms of old age—ways you feel now that you did not feel when younger.
2. Discuss biblical examples of men and women who accomplished great things when older.
3. Why is it important to stay busy in your senior years?
4. Discuss the opportunity and the necessity of prayer at all ages, but especially as we grow older.
5. Discuss a history of retirement and why there are some areas of our life from which we can never retire.
6. How many people retire each day in the U.S.? What impact does that have on our culture?
7. Name several good secular examples of people who accomplished great things in their older age.
8. Is *retirement* a biblical word?
9. Is retirement a biblical requirement?
10. Are you content at your current age?

CHAPTER 2

THE SOUL

A Little Humor—You Know You're Getting Older When
Everything hurts, and what doesn't hurt, doesn't work. You feel like the morning after, and you didn't even go anywhere the night before. Your knees buckle, and your belt won't. You can only burn the midnight oil until 9:00. The twinkle in your eye is the sun hitting your bifocals. Your back goes out more often than you do. And another surefire way of knowing you're getting older is when your birthday rolls around once again and you really don't feel like celebrating.

Most Important
It is no wonder that because of the immediacy of needs in the physical world, we give so little attention to the most important part of a human being: the soul. From the moment we come into this world, we face pressures to meet the physical needs of life just to sustain it, to grow, to become educated, to become social, to procreate, and to rear our families. It is only as we approach the senior years that we seemingly have the time to begin to consider what is most important in our lives. During the first part of our lives, education, courtship and marriage, career, and family all press on us with unrelenting urgency. But as years pass, and we retire from the pressures of work, the children leave the nest, we may be blessed with grandchildren who come and (thankfully) go, and our need and even desire for material things lessens, we realize that there is less life left for us than has already passed. Our physical life is short at best. James says it is a "vapor" that

CHAPTER 2

appears for a little time and vanishes (4:14). As that vapor becomes thinner and thinner as we age, we begin to think about "Where do we go from here. What's next?" Some are able to dismiss the thought and say, "I'll just let what will be will be." Others take a more serious approach and begin to look at what God's Word says about the soul and its eternal nature. Our time on earth is but a speck compared to eternity, yet what we do *here* prepares us for *there*. Instead of giving up, giving in, slowing down, and retiring from what's most important—our spiritual nature—we should be increasingly occupying our newfound time with thoughts of more immediate preparation for the life to come. The more spiritual and involved in God's work we are in our younger years, the easier the transition as we grow older.

Though the soul is the most important part of us, most of our attention is given to our bodies. Our bodies are important; they are the temple of the Holy Spirit and our soul. We spend so much money on our personal appearance, don't we? Look at all the resources we dole out for our clothes, cosmetics, exercise, and any product that promises to make us look or feel younger. But Jesus constantly called attention to the soul, the eternal part of man. How often do we consider the value of our soul and the price that was paid for it? How often do we think about the importance of other people's souls—relatives, friends, or even strangers? Jesus, in His life and death, is proof positive of the worth of our soul. Jesus tells us just how important the soul is. In Matthew 16:26, "For what will it profit a man if he gains the whole world and loses or forfeits his soul? Or what shall a man give in return for his soul?" Nothing is more important than the soul of man. No amount of money or worldly possessions is more important than an eternal unseen part of every one of us. Unfortunately, there are many who sell their souls for virtually nothing. They lie and steal for a little bit of material gain or advantage. Some sell their bodies into prostitution, both male and female, for a small amount of money compared to the eternal value of the soul. Many more rob, steal, and even murder to profit in one way or another from their foul actions. Yes, most people place little value on their soul. Most are unaware they have a soul, or if they do know, they don't care. How unwise and short-sighted to live only for this world and the meager crumbs it can give us compared to eternity with the God who created everything and wants to bless us with all good things.

All material things will perish. Only the spiritual qualities will survive. What if a person could be given a title or ownership of the entire world? It really would be of little value long-term because everything we see, feel, smell, taste, or experience is temporary. Solomon concluded by saying, "All is vanity" (Ecclesiastes 1:14). As we compare the value of the soul with any or all material assets, we need to remember this life is like a flower that fades away (James 1:11). We need to realize the folly of the rich fool in Luke 12:15-21, and we need to consider the bad judgment of the rich man in the story of Lazarus (Luke 16:19-31). Life is short at best; eternity is forever (Romans 6:23), and we prepare here for there.

There is a high price to be paid for losing our soul. Although the body is important, the soul is the most valuable possession we have. It is the eternal part of us. Its existence is not terminated when the body dies. The soul is also valuable because of what it cost to redeem it—the life of the Son of God. "What can anyone give in exchange for their soul?" (Matthew 16:26, NIV). The word *exchange* carries with it the idea of a business transaction in which we are bartering or bargaining for something. *Bartering* means to trade or exchange one commodity for another. If the devil came to us—and he does—as he did to Jesus in the wilderness and began to barter with us for our soul, I wonder what it would take for him to gain possession of your soul. A million? Ten million? Half a million? A hundred thousand? How much money would it take?

CHAPTER 2

Unfortunately, many sell their souls for almost nothing. I hope we truly understand its value. Some sell their souls for material things. Some sell their souls for sensual pleasures or pride and power. Others are led away from God by false teachings because they simply have never read God's Word or understood it well enough to say, "Be gone, Satan! For it is written…" (Matthew 4:10, ESV). Still others have never put forth the slightest bit of effort to find out what it would take to save their soul. Although it is the most valuable possession we have, its salvation is free. We can't buy it or earn it, but we can accept the mercy and grace of God, seeking to do His will every day as grateful recipients of the most precious gift of all—eternal life with God. It doesn't matter how much money you may acquire in your lifetime, or how much pleasure you may have, or what crazy idea you may come up with that is completely out of step with God's Word and will, or whether you go through this life carelessly, living for the moment, never studying God's Word, never learning what He wants or expects of us, and therefore never achieving your real purpose. We can't afford to lose our soul. We know our bodies are going to die. We know that placing an emphasis entirely upon our bodies is misspent effort, but taking care of the soul and laying up treasure in heaven is where the greatest eternal benefits are paid (Matthew 6:21).

> "Be faithful unto death, and I will give you the crown of life" (Revelation 2:10).

The Decline of the Body, the Rise of the Spirit—and Soul

"So we do not lose heart. Though our outer self is wasting away, our inner self is being renewed day by day" (2 Corinthians 4:16). It is the natural order of things, or maybe we should say, "It's the way it's *supposed* to be." As we get older, the body declines. But our spirit, our soul, should become more mature, and we should become more like God.

The Body Dies—The Soul Returns to God

> In the day when the keepers of the house tremble, and the strong men are bent, and the grinders cease because they are few, and those who look through the window are dimmed, and the doors on the street are shut—when the sound of the grinding is low, and one rises up at the sound of a bird, and all the daughters of song are brought low—they are afraid also of what is high, and terrors are in the way; the almond tree blossoms, the grasshopper drags itself along, and desire fails, because man is going to his eternal home, and the mourners go about the streets—before the silver cord is snapped, or the golden bowl is broken, or the pitcher is shattered at the fountain, or the wheel broken at the cistern, and the dust returns to the earth as it was, and the spirit returns to God who gave it (Ecclesiastes 12:3-7).

What an incredible ancient description of the aging process! An interpretation of this passage is interesting. Our bodies will grow feeble, our teeth will decay, our eyesight will fail (verse 3). There is no doubt that some things become more difficult as we age. Arthritis, the wearing out of joints, the loss of mobility, our diminishing eyesight, and even the need to get false teeth all speak of the aging process. Verse 4: The noisy grinding of grain will be shut out by the deaf ear—the inability to hear well. But even the songs of a bird will keep us awake at night. Verse 5: A person will be afraid to climb up a hill or walk down a road for fear of obstacles (fear of falling). One's hair will turn white as the almond blossom, and one will feel lifeless and drag along like the grasshopper. In time we each go to our eternal home, and the streets are filled with those who mourn.

The DNA of our bodies is that it will wear out sooner or later. It was never designed to last forever. And as we experience the aging process, we will notice subtle changes. Because of the design of the body, it is a challenge to grow older with grace and dignity. We must have realistic expectations. Circumstances will tell us it is time to slow down in certain areas and concentrate on others.

CHAPTER 2

We should not overstate the issue. By taking care of ourselves, eating well, getting enough sleep, avoiding all of the sure killers (such as indulgence in alcohol, tobacco, or other drugs, and the lack of reasonable exercise), we cannot only extend our lives a little, but can make our lives more comfortable as we continue to age.

Self Control—God Control

We also understand as we grow older that self control is absolutely essential in all areas of our life. We are to live "self-controlled, upright, and godly lives in the present age" (Titus 2:12). If we can apply self-control physically, mentally, and spiritually, it will help make the aging process easier. Age is an issue of mind over matter. If you don't mind, it doesn't matter! We need to mind more about the good, eternal things of life.

It is important that we maintain self-control in emotional areas as well. We need to learn how to be emotionally self-controlled and not given to emotional extremes. Thomas Aldrich, a well-known writer, said, "To keep the heart unwrinkled, to be helpful, kindly, cheerful, reverent—that is to triumph over older age." Moderation and balance in all things help as we go down life's path and help protect our souls. Remember, maintaining a good sense of humor is absolutely essential to successfully growing old gracefully. It was Groucho Marx who said, "I intend to live forever, or die trying." He also said, "I have always been taught to respect my elders, and have reached the age where I have none left to respect." Michael Pritchard said, "You don't stop laughing because you grow old, but you grow older because you stop laughing." I like this accurate observation from Australian writer Rita Joseph, "It's curious as we grow older how easy it is to lose our sense of direction, a sense of vocation, a sense of God, calling us to important things still to be done. Vocations are not just for the young starting out in a marriage or a career or religious life. There is another kind of vocation, a kind of late vocation—*God's final call to a strong finish.* It is God's call to each one of us to grow old gracefully, full of grace, to grow toward Him. God calls us to respond heroically like Paul, pouring ourselves out like a libation [drink offering] until we can say: 'I have fought the good fight, I have finished the race, I have kept the faith' (2 Timothy 4:7). As our bodies grow older and more frail, our souls are to grow stronger and more true. That is our final vocation, and it is worth contemplating every day for the rest of our life. When all is said and done, it is the last call that really counts."

Self-control can only be accomplished by allowing God to take control of our lives.

Blessed in Aging
By Esther Mary Walker

Blessed are they who understand
My faltering step and shaking hand
Blessed, who know my ears today
Must strain to hear the things they say.
Blessed are those who seem to know
My eyes are dim and my mind is slow
Blessed are those who look away
When I spilled tea that weary day.

Blessed are they who, with cheery smile
Stopped to chat for a little while
Blessed are they who know the way
To bring back memories of yesterday.

Blessed are those who never say
"You've told that story twice today"
Blessed are they who make it known
That I am loved, respected, and not alone.

And blessed are they who will ease the days
Of my journey home, in loving ways.

CHAPTER 2

There are wonderful passages of Scripture that give us inspiration and encourage us to age with grace:

"Gray hair is a crown of glory; it is gained in a righteous life" (Proverbs 16:31).

"...even to your old age I am he, and to gray hairs I will carry you. I have made, and I will bear; I will carry and will save" (Isaiah 46:4).

"The righteous flourish like the palm tree and grow like a cedar in Lebanon. They are planted in the house of the Lord; they flourish in the courts of our God. *They still bear fruit in old age*; they are ever full of sap and green, to declare that the Lord is upright; he is my rock, and there is no unrighteousness in him" (Psalm 92:12-15).

"You shall stand up before the gray head and honor the face of an old man, and you shall fear your God: I am the Lord" (Leviticus 19:32).

"The glory of young men is their strength, but the splendor of old men is their gray hair" (Proverbs 20:29).

"But if anyone does not provide for his relatives, and especially for members of his household, he has denied the faith and is worse than an unbeliever" (1 Timothy 5:8).

Which simply means that we need to take care of our younger and older family members;

"Honor your father and your mother, that your days may be long in the land that the Lord your God is giving you" (Exodus 20:12).

" Whoever seeks to preserve his life will lose it, but whosoever loses it will keep it" (Luke 17:33).

"Listen to your father who gave you life, and do not despise your mother when she is old" (Proverbs 23:22).

Not For Sissies

Someone has said, "Old age is not for sissies." As the years go by, that statement becomes clearer. We have to be strong and courageous and willing to faithfully struggle so that we may adequately make it through our older years. Physical, mental, and even spiritual challenges seem to come with increasing speed as we grow older.

What Is the Condition of Your Soul?
It does not matter what you accomplish in this world. If you lose your soul, you have failed. You may have amassed great wealth or achieved fame; you may have thousands to mourn at your funeral; but if you have lost your soul, you have lost everything!

Conversely, you may die alone in poverty and be buried in an unmarked grave, but if your soul has been saved by the grace of God through Jesus, you are among the richest to have ever lived.

It is the love of God and the death of Jesus that allows us to be bought back from sin and spiritual death. Read the following New Testament statement passages:

> "For while we were still weak, at the right time Christ died for the ungodly. For one will scarcely die for a righteous person—though perhaps for a good person one would dare even to die—but God shows his love for us in that while we were still sinners, Christ died for us" (Romans 5:6-8).

> "Knowing that you were ransomed from the futile ways inherited from your forefathers, not with perishable things such as silver or gold, but with the precious blood of Christ, like that of a lamb without blemish or spot. He was foreknown before the foundation of the world but was made manifest in the last times for the sake of you" (1 Peter 1:18-20).

> "No one can serve two masters, for either he will hate the one and love the other, or he will be devoted to the one and despise the other. You cannot serve God and money. Therefore I tell you, do not be anxious about your life, what you will eat or what you will drink, nor about your body, what you will put on. Is not life more than food, and the body more than clothing?" (Matthew 6:24, 25).

CHAPTER 2

"What shall we say then? Are we to continue in sin that grace may abound? By no means! How can we who died to sin still live in it? Do you not know that all of us who have been baptized into Christ Jesus were baptized into his death? We were buried therefore with him by baptism into death, in order that, just as Christ was raised from the dead by the glory of the Father, we too might walk in newness of life" (Romans 6:1-4).

Questions

1. What is the most important part of every human being, and what is its primary importance?
2. Do we give the most attention and importance to that part of us? Why or why not?
3. Discuss Matthew 16:26 and how it relates to each of us.
4. What was Solomon's conclusion as to what is most important for man?
5. Discuss the concept that as our bodies decline, our spiritual nature should increase (2 Corinthians 4:16).
6. Read and discuss Ecclesiastes 12:3-7.
7. How can we as Christians finish our race well?
8. Read and discuss Psalm 92:12-15.
9. Does the commission in 1 Timothy 5:8 of providing for our families apply to older members as well as younger ones?
10. As a maturing Christian, what is the current condition of your soul?

CHAPTER 3

MATURITY

A Little Humor

It seems that lately as I am getting older my life has been getting more complicated, and I want to thank those of you who are brave enough to still associate with me regardless of what I have become. The following is a recap of my current identity:

- I am a fiscal and moral conservative, which makes me a fascist. I am heterosexual, which makes me a homophobe.
- I am a Christian, which makes me an infidel.
- I am older than 70 and retired, which makes me a useless old person.
- I think and I reason; therefore I doubt much that the media tells me, which makes me a reactionary.
- I am proud of my heritage and our inclusive American culture, which makes me a xenophobe.
- I value my safety and that of my family; therefore I appreciate the police and the legal system, which makes me a right-wing extremist.
- I believe in hard work, fair play, and fair compensation according to each individual's merits, which makes me anti-social.
- I, and my friends my age, acquired a good education without student loans and no debt at graduation, which makes me some kind of odd underachiever.
- I believe in the defense and protection of the homeland by all citizens, which makes me a militarist.

CHAPTER 3

Please help me come to terms with this, because I'm not sure who I am anymore! My latest problem…I'm not sure which bathroom I should use. (Unknown)

Wisdom

> "But the wisdom from above is first pure, then peaceable, gentle, open to reason, full of mercy and good fruits, impartial and sincere. And a harvest of righteousness is sown in peace by those who make peace" (James 3:17, 18).

We all come into this world as infants. We need to be taken care of and provided for in every way. But as we grow and develop, we begin the maturing process. After a while we no longer need to be fed. We can feed ourselves. We no longer need to be bathed. We can bathe ourselves. And so the maturing process continues until we get to the point where we can take care of ourselves, meeting our own needs. Maturity is an important process.

In every area of our lives, there is the need for maturity—physical, mental, emotional, and especially spiritual. Many feel that youth is good, but maturity may be better, and in many ways it is. When we look to nature, it often takes seven or eight years for fruit trees to mature, bloom, and produce. A watermelon, when it is red, juicy, and mature, is at its best. A rose in full bloom is most beautiful. The giant oak tree, as it grows and develops a tall and wide canopy, offers refreshing shade. A properly aged steak is more delicious. A mature Christian is a wonderful example of a life well lived!

Maturity has its benefits as well as liabilities. Many people are slow to mature or develop. The greatest accomplishments of their lives are in their older age after they have developed much wisdom and understanding and have learned to profit from their past mistakes. One of the saddest things to observe is a person who either physically, mentally, or emotionally never matures. In some respects, he or she remains a child. But the most devastating and eternally consequential sadness is to see an older person who is still spiritually a child.

Paul spoke of the fact that when we first become Christians we are all babes in Christ. We have to be fed milk rather than meat (1 Corinthians 3:2). There are certain things we cannot digest or understand because of our newness in Christ. But as we grow older, we should mature in every spiritual respect. As we grow, we feed upon God's Word (Acts 20:32) and begin to understand the more difficult passages of Scripture. Hopefully we develop a spiritual appetite, and hunger and thirst for righteousness (Matthew 5:6). Spiritual infants are those who cease to grow after becoming a Christian. These spiritual infants are always more concerned with themselves than in helping others and being of service. Unfortunately, spiritual infants are often more concerned with arguing or complaining than they are in positive actions, and are often easily led in the wrong direction. They have not been fed the word of the Spirit and have not "grown in the grace and knowledge of our Lord Jesus Christ." Hopefully we can mature so we can leave behind the more elementary elements of our Christian walk and begin to fully understand that to be a Christian is to be a servant. To be a Christian is to make sacrifices. To be mature is to grow in faith.

> We should grow until we all attain to the unity of the faith and of the knowledge of the Son of God, to mature manhood, to the measure of the stature of the fullness of Christ, so that we may no longer be children, tossed to and fro by the waves and carried about by every wind of doctrine, by human cunning, by craftiness in deceitful schemes. Rather, speaking the truth in love, we are to grow up in every way into him who is the head, into Christ...to put off your old self, which belongs to your former manner of life and is corrupt through deceitful desires, and to be renewed in the spirit of your minds, and to put on the new self, created after the likeness of God in true righteousness and holiness.
>
> Therefore, having put away falsehood, let each one of you speak the truth with his neighbor, for we are members one of another. Be angry and do not sin; do not let the sun go down on your

anger, and give no opportunity to the devil…. Let all bitterness and wrath and anger and clamor and slander be put away from you, along with all malice. Be kind to one another, tenderhearted, forgiving one another, as God in Christ forgave you (Ephesians 4:13-15, 22-32).

Here Paul gives us a beautiful synopsis of true maturity.

Evidences of Maturity
Wisdom

"Blessed is the one who finds wisdom" (Proverbs 3:13).

The word blessed means "happy, complete." Wisdom is one of the primary evidences of Christian maturity. It allows us to use all of our talents and all of the experience of our lives to make good decisions, and it allows us to avoid the pitfalls and snares along life's road. True wisdom helps us to use our time wisely. Instead of wasting it, we use it to the benefit of others and to the glory of God. A mature Christian will become wise!

There are two kinds of wisdom. One is earthly wisdom; that is, the wisdom of the world. This comes about often by personal experience. If we depend on this kind of wisdom, however, we are going to make many mistakes and experience much pain. It's a life of trial and error, repeating mistakes over and over again until we finally catch on to the pain and waste involved.

The second and more beneficial kind of wisdom is the wisdom of God, the wisdom that comes from above. The earlier we learn to study and understand God's Word and put it into practical application in our lives, the more effective we will become in our quest for wisdom. Many younger people are wiser than some who are older, simply because they have studied and understood what God's Word teaches, applied it, and experienced its benefits. With the wisdom we learn from studying God's Word, it is possible to grow old gracefully.

The Results of Spiritual Wisdom

Spiritual wisdom allows us to know what to do with the knowledge we have. It allows us to know the real source of wisdom.

> "If any of you lacks wisdom, let him ask God, who gives generously to all without reproach, and it will be given him" (James 1:5).

Mature spiritual wisdom wants to know what the will of God is, understand His will, and then apply it to our life in every way. We should seek the will of God each day. The duties we read about in God's Word become our desires. Instead of *having* to do something the Word teaches, we sincerely *want* to do it because we know it is what's best. That is true spiritual wisdom.

> "But the wisdom from above is first pure, then peaceable, gentle, open to reason, full of mercy and good fruits, impartial and sincere" (James 3:17).

The true Christian wants to submit to the will of God voluntarily, "as the church submits to Christ" (Ephesians 5:24). We read of "Submitting to one another" in Ephesians 5:21 and, of course, a part of that is first submitting ourselves to God. Submission to the will of God and preferring one another over self is the opposite of rebellion and being self-willed. It is one of the true tests of Christian maturity. The true Christian learns the meaning of love—to love God first and our fellow man as we love ourselves. As mature Christians, we become ambassadors for Christ wherever we go. Hopefully when people see us, they see Jesus living in us. As we speak, our words are comforting and encouraging, and our acts are kind and thoughtful. It is difficult to take self-inventory, to see where we are in the maturing process. A good question each of us could ask ourselves right now would be, "How spiritually mature am I?"

Evidences of Growing Older in God's Wisdom

First Timothy 4 gives us a kind of checklist of how we are doing in our maturing process.

CHAPTER 3

Verse 12: "Set the believers an example in speech, in conduct, in love, in faith, in purity." Every person has a reputation and is an example to others, either good or bad. The mature Christian will be mostly a good example.

Verse 13: "Until I come, devote yourself to the public reading of Scripture, to exhortation, to teaching." It is essential for the mature, wise Christian to study to "present [himself] to God as one approved, a worker who has no need to be ashamed, rightly handling the word of truth" (2 Timothy 2:15). We need to study daily and feed on God's Word so that we may become strong. What we feed grows; what we starve dies. How long has it been since we studied God's Word individually? Are we failing in our daily walk because we do not know the Scriptures and are unable to resist the temptations of Satan as a result of this ignorance? If we study God's Word, it is a guarantee that we will have a regular infusion of God's wisdom.

Verse 14: "Do not neglect the gift you have." Each of us has unique talents, abilities, and opportunities. God has given these to us, and here we are told not to neglect them, but to use them. An unused talent, ability, or opportunity is completely useless, but if we are using the gifts that God has given us, then He will allow us more opportunities and increased degrees of talent. How sad it is to see people with great abilities and talents never using them in God's kingdom! But it's so encouraging to see those who may only have one or two talents, but who are using them daily and effectively to God's glory.

Finally in verses 15 and 16, he says, "Practice these things, immerse yourself in them, so that all may see your progress. Keep a close watch on yourself and on the teaching. Persist in this, for by so doing you will save both yourself and your hearers." We have a responsibility to ourselves and to others. One of the greatest marks of maturity is perseverance, not giving up—when the going gets tough, we get going!

As we get older, almost everything becomes more difficult. It becomes harder to get up, get ready, and go to worship or Bible study. It becomes harder to visit or to fulfill many Christian responsibilities and opportunities that are ours. But perseverance and doing what we can as long as we can are two of the great evidences of Christian maturity and wisdom. When we get extremely sick or disabled, there is no doubt that God understands. But even then, we may be able to shift our attention to writing cards, making phone calls, or to spending more time in prayer for others.

Second Peter 1:3-11 is a comforting passage for those of us growing older in the faith. It emphasizes various qualities that we will possess if we are adequately maturing:

> "His divine power has granted to us all things that pertain to life and godliness, through the knowledge of him who called us to his own glory and excellence, by which he has granted to us his precious and very great promises, so that through them you may become partakers of the divine nature, having escaped from the corruption that is in the world because of sinful desire. For this very reason, make every effort to supplement your faith with virtue, and virtue with knowledge, and knowledge with self-control, and self-control with steadfastness, and steadfastness with godliness, and godliness with brotherly affection, and brotherly affection with love. For if these qualities are yours and are increasing, they keep you from being ineffective or unfruitful in the knowledge of our Lord Jesus Christ. For whoever lacks these qualities is so nearsighted that he is blind, having forgotten that he was cleansed from his former sins. Therefore, brothers, be all the more diligent to confirm your calling and election, for if you practice these qualities you will never fall. For in this way there will be richly provided for you an entrance into the eternal kingdom of our Lord and Savior Jesus Christ."

Virtue is the determination to do right. *Knowledge* is the knowledge of God's Word as it tells us what is right. *Self-control*

CHAPTER 3

is applying the knowledge to our life, also referred to as wisdom. *Perseverance* (or steadfastness) means remaining faithful to the very end. Godliness is the goal of the Christian: to become as much like God through Jesus Christ as we can. *Godliness* is demonstrated by being kind to one another, tenderhearted toward brethren, being devoted to God and our fellow man, and seeking to do God's will in everything.

Another excellent checklist for our maturity level is the fruit of the Spirit. Galatians 5:22-24: "But the fruit of the Spirit is love, joy, peace, patience, kindness, goodness, faithfulness, gentleness, self-control; against such things there is no law. And those who belong to Christ Jesus have crucified the flesh with its passions and desires." Wow! What a litmus test for maturity and wisdom!

Paul, in Titus 2:7, 8, gives a short, but complete definition of Christian maturity and how it is observed by others. "Show yourself in all respects to be a model of good works, and in your teaching show integrity, dignity, and sound speech that cannot be condemned, so that an opponent may be put to shame, having nothing evil to say about us," Many of these qualities are so important that they are repeated in various passages.

In his letter to Titus, Paul gives us a good description of maturity and wisdom in older men and women. "Older men [those of us who are senior citizens] are to be sober-minded, dignified, self-controlled, sound in faith, in love, and in steadfastness." Then he shifts to the maturity of older women. "Older women likewise are to be reverent in behavior, not slanderers or slaves to much wine. They are to teach what is good, and so train the young women to love their husbands and children, to be self-controlled, pure, working at home, kind, and submissive to their own husbands, that the word of God may not be reviled" (Titus 2:1-6). In these verses, Paul gets specific as to how we are to mature as older Christian men and women. Sometimes the most difficult part of growing older is to admit where we are in the aging process and simply to behave as mature, wise, Christian men and women.

A Closer Look

Concerning the older men Paul says they are to be "sound of mind" or "sober minded" (Titus 2:2). They should have a healthy mind that is not polluted by the world. In this passage, Paul is encouraging Titus to be straightforward toward the people of Crete. They were an immoral and worldly people, and by this point, they had been converted to Christ. These qualities that Paul gave to Titus are the exact opposite to that which the Cretans had been accustomed most of their lives. They were to have control over their mind in that they did not rush to judgment or make quick decisions.

The stability of the church and its effectiveness and influence in the community and the actual health of the church is to a large extent dependent on those who are older. Children, young people, and young adults all have a vital role in the church, but those who are older set the tone for the church. They have wisdom and experience, and mature gifts and talents. They have resources, financial and otherwise, that the church desperately needs. Many older Christians have much to offer, and are looking for opportunities to serve in the church. So what Paul tells Titus to teach the older men is important, even essential. We must possess certain qualities to ensure that those same qualities live on in the church. Thus, we must be temperate, sober-minded, sensible, and mature. Paul goes on to say that these older men are to be worthy of respect. There is a difference between demanding respect and being worthy of respect. It is unfortunate that not all older people are worthy of respect. Some are self-centered, demanding, and proud, even lustful and bad-tempered. Paul warns Titus against such behavior.

The older men are also to be self-controlled. When we are self-controlled, we are able to make wise decisions. We are ethical, in that we keep our word and that what we say is reflected in what we do. Our actions and reactions are under control. This does not mean that we are to be somber and never smile or laugh. It just means that we are able to distinguish between a time to be serious and a time for levity and humor. A self-controlled person knows the difference in what is appropriate and what isn't.

Next, Paul mentions that older Christian men are to be sound in the faith, in love, and in patience (endurance or steadfastness). These characteristics are essential if older men are to be the proper example to a younger generation. A strong faith, a deep love, and patience or endurance will serve anyone well in their quest for Christian maturity. Without biblical love, it is easy to become cynical, critical, and have a fault-finding disposition—even to become hard of heart and unnecessarily stubborn. Some become like the man who had been in the church for 45 years. Someone said to him, "You must have really seen a lot of changes during your time." The man replied, "I sure have, and I have opposed every one of them!" Having endurance or patience doesn't mean putting up with what is wrong or overlooking sin or error. It does mean that we do not allow ourselves to become weak or to be tempted to give up or just lose interest in God's Word and will. It means we are faithful until death.

There are all kinds of ministries in which older people can become involved. These include phoning or visiting those who are sick, writing cards, and praying for those in need every day, asking God's blessings upon them.

Responsibilities of Older Women

Older women have a unique and vitally important role in the church. Paul says they are to be "reverent." It is because they have a high calling and important responsibility. Their reverence should be evidenced by the way they live—their dress, their conversation, and their actions. This behavior should be consistent whether they're at home, in public, or at church.

Paul says they should not be "slanderers." Slander is unfair, unkind, usually untrue, and quite harmful. No good comes from it. It is often done away from the person being slandered so that they do not have an opportunity to defend themselves. As a result of this kind of behavior, people's reputations are ruined and often innocent people suffer because of the lies (or half-truths) of others. We would all be better off if we would make sure that our attitude, our speech, and our actions are positive, uplifting, and devoid of unsubstantiated or unnecessary criticism. If you want to split a church, start slandering other members.

The next quality mentioned by Paul is not "slaves to much wine" (Titus 2:3). In Crete, it may have been the custom for the women to sit around, drinking wine and gossiping. Certainly when we use any substance that causes us to be impaired or to use bad judgment, we should give that substance up immediately. Our minds should be controlled by the Spirit of God and His Word, not by an impairing substance.

Paul then turns his attention to more positive instructions. The older women are to teach or "train the young women to love their husbands and children." I am convinced we can learn to love more fully. We can learn to be a better husband, wife, or parent. Paul says love is a learning process, and there are evidences of love that must be taught and demonstrated.

One would think this would be easy, needing little to no instruction. Yet what can be taught can be learned, and there are some people who need to be taught the meaning of the word *love*, even to love their children. Too many parents indulge their children, never correcting them, never teaching them, never setting proper examples for them. To behave in this manner is the essence of not loving them. Love always seeks the best interest of the person being loved.

Next, Paul says that the older women are to teach the younger women to be "self-controlled." Just as older men must be self-

CHAPTER 3

controlled, so older women must possess this quality to pass it on to the younger women.

Self-control is essential for all of us. We need to exercise self-control in how we speak, eat, or dress, or what we read, watch on TV, or post on social media. We should use self-control in speaking to our spouse or children. Purity is part of the package. It is a virtue and needs to be taught.

This next point may be controversial. Paul writes that the younger women should be "working at home." Most women I know are extremely busy at home, even those who work at a full-time job. They have their paid job, and then they go home and do all the necessary things to keep the household running. Recently I have noticed that more and more couples are opting for the wife to stay home and be a literal homemaker rather than enjoying the benefits of two salaries. In some instances it may be necessary that the mother or wife work, but when possible, the home functions better when the mother is there full-time.

The next principle that older women are to teach younger women is to be kind. This is best taught by example, but certainly it has to be verbalized, as well. A kind personality is one of the most attractive qualities a person can develop.

Finally, younger women are to be taught to be "submissive to their own husbands." If a husband truly loves his wife and is reasonable and fair with her, this should never be a problem. But if the husband is unfair and fails to follow the commandments of the Lord, then this issue will always create problems. Just as God is the head of Jesus, and Jesus is the head of the church, so the husband is to be the head of the home. The most important part of this is that the husband is to set proper examples and maintain proper dispositions both toward his wife and his children. If he carries out this responsibility in a godly manner, there will be few problems in the home. This is a command of God and must be taught and followed.

Food for Thought

"…and the advantage of knowledge is that wisdom preserves the life of him who has it" (Ecclesiastes 7:12).

"The fear of the Lord is the beginning of wisdom; all those who practice it have a good understanding. His praise endures forever!" (Psalm 111:10).

"Blessed is the one who finds wisdom, and the one who gets understanding, for the gain from her is better than gain from silver and her profit better than gold. She is more precious than jewels, and nothing you desire can compare with her. Long life is in her right hand; in her left hand are riches and honor. Her ways are ways of pleasantness, and all her paths are peace. She is a tree of life to those who lay hold of her; those who hold her fast are called blessed" (Proverbs 3:13-18).

"My son, do not lose sight of these—keep sound wisdom and discretion, and they will be life for your soul and adornment for your neck. Then you will walk on your way securely, and your foot will not stumble. If you lie down, you will not be afraid; when you lie down, your sleep will be sweet. Do not be afraid of sudden terror or of the ruin of the wicked, when it comes, for the Lord will be your confidence and will keep your foot from being caught" (Proverbs 3:21-26).

"So teach us to number our days that we may get a heart of wisdom" (Psalm 90:12).

"They still bear fruit in old age; they are ever full of sap and green" (Psalm 92:14).

"You are my hiding place and my shield; I hope in your word" (Psalm 119:114).

"So if a person lives many years, let him rejoice in them all; but let him remember that the days of darkness will be many…." (Ecclesiastes 11:8).

CHAPTER 3

Questions

1. Discuss how wisdom should be an integral part of the maturing process.
2. How do some people remain children spiritually rather than growing and maturing normally (1 Corinthians 3:2)?
3. What are we to feed upon to gain the spiritual strength we need for spiritual development?
4. What are some symptoms of Christians remaining spiritually immature?
5. How is wisdom one of the evidences of Christian maturity?
6. What are the two kinds of wisdom discussed in the Bible?
7. What are some of the evidences of Christians developing wisdom in the maturing process?
8. What are some requirements given for older Christian men (Titus 2:7, 8)?
9. What are responsibilities of mature Christian women?
10. Are you pleased with your current level of maturity and wisdom?

CHAPTER 4

FORGETTING THE PAST

A Little Sobering Humor

A man of 92 years, short, very well-presented, who takes great care in his appearance, is moving into an old people's home today. His wife of 70 years has recently died, and he is obliged to leave his home.

After waiting several hours in the retirement home lobby, he gently smiles as he is told his room is ready. As he slowly walks to the elevator, using his cane, I describe the small room to him, including the sheet hung at the window which serves as a curtain.

"I like it very much," he says, with the enthusiasm of an 8-year-old boy who has just been given a new puppy.

"Sir, you haven't even seen the room yet. Hang on a moment, we are almost there."

"That has nothing to do with it," he replies. "Happiness is something I choose in advance. Whether or not I like the room does not depend on the furniture, or the décor. Rather, it depends on how I decide to see it. It is already decided in my mind that I like my room. It is a decision I make every morning when I wake up. I can choose. I can spend my day in bed enumerating all the difficulties that I have with the parts of my body that no longer work very well, or I can get up and give thanks to heaven for those parts that are still in working order. Every day is a gift, and as long as I can open my eyes, I will focus on the new day and all the happy memories that I have built up during my life. Old age is like a bank account. You withdraw in later life what you have deposited along the way."

CHAPTER 4

So, my advice to you is to deposit all the happiness you can in your bank account of memories. Thank you for your part in filling my account with happy memories, which I am still continuing to fill.

Remember these simple guidelines for happiness:

1. Free your heart from hate.
2. Free your mind from worry.
3. Live simple.
4. Give more.
5. Expect less.   (source unknown)

There are several dangers in living in the past. One is that we keep repeating, to anyone who will listen, all of the accomplishments of our life. As we get older, there is a great temptation to show off or highlight all of the victories and important events in our life. I am sure you have met people who tell you the same stories over and over again about their exploits in one area or another. It is as if they are stuck in the past. I know men in their 60s and 70s who still wear ponytails, earrings, and listen to the Grateful Dead. They are stuck in the 1960s. I know others who are stuck in the '40s and '50s, recounting over and over again their World War II, Korean, or Vietnam War stories. And it isn't that these memories are not important. They are. But getting stuck in the past and having these as our primary positive memories is dangerous and may even send the wrong message to our children, grandchildren, and others who hear them over and over again.

Then there is another danger; that is, we dwell on the mistakes of the past, allowing them to prevent us from using our talents and abilities in the present. We tell people that God will forgive all sins except our denying God and His Son Jesus as the Son of God. Yet many people live as if they have committed some unforgivable sin even though they know their past sins are forgiven, but then they slip back again into a feeling of failure and inability to let go of that past sin for which they have received forgiveness.

There are many people who are so bound by their prior transgressions and sins that they are unable to use their God-given talents and abilities in the present. How sad! How many people have failed to preach or teach or share with other individuals their Christian faith simply because they feel unworthy due to past sins. Not forgetting our past sins and transgressions is an albatross around our neck, which will limit our present and future. Not letting go of our past can either be caused by pride and arrogance, because of our perceived successes and accomplishments, or it can be due to our failures and losses.

When Paul said, "I am going to forget the past," he was doing so because of his successes and failures. Can you imagine having been chosen by God while still a young man to be His primary spokesman to those of the New Covenant? Paul was one of the most educated young Jewish men of his day. He was conscientious and aggressive in his faith. He knew and kept the old law religiously. He was, no doubt, destined for greatness in the Jewish faith.

> "Indeed, I count everything as loss because of the surpassing worth of knowing Christ Jesus my Lord. For his sake I have suffered the loss of all things and count them as rubbish, in order that I may gain Christ" (Philippians 3:8).

> "Not that I have already obtained this or am already perfect, but I press on to make it my own, because Christ Jesus has made me his own. Brothers, I do not consider that I have made it my own. But one thing I do: forgetting what lies behind and straining forward to what lies ahead, I press on toward the goal for the prize of the upward call of God in Christ Jesus" (Philippians 3:12-14).

> "Finally, brothers, whatever is true, whatever is honorable, whatever is just, whatever is pure, whatever is lovely, whatever is commendable, if there is any excellence, if there is anything worthy of praise, think about these things. What you have learned and received and heard and seen in me—practice these things, and the God of peace will be with you" (Philippians 4:8,9).

CHAPTER 4

We should not live in the past, either regretting our mistakes and sins and missed opportunities or reminiscing and bragging about our major accomplishments in the past, whether they be war stories, business successes, sports accomplishments, or other achievements. To live mostly in the past is dangerous. It takes our eyes off the present and the future. It makes it likely that we will get off track. Looking back is usually a discouraging or prideful experience. Looking back can cause depression and anxiety. Looking back can cause us defeat in the future, limiting us in doing our best in the present because of the regrets or successes of the past.

Concerning this, Jesus said, "No one who puts his hand to the plow and looks back is fit for the kingdom of God" (Luke 9:62). Any farmer, ancient or modern, using a mule or a tractor, knows that if you are plowing a field and you spend your time looking back, you are going to veer off to the left or right. This distraction will cause you to end up in the wrong place. If you are driving a car and you are constantly looking back, you will either cross the center line or run off the shoulder of the road. You may crash into another car or an obstacle on the side of the road. Looking back causes us to take our eyes off our destination.

Most of us, if we are honest, do not see a pleasant picture when we look back on our past. Our sins and bad judgments are obvious throughout our past. In our past, we often concentrated on self, were captivated by greed, and were often selfish. But for those of us who are Christians, we have been blessed with forgiveness, cleansing, and healing by the grace of God through Jesus Christ. Looking back keeps us from realizing the best is yet to come because of the blessings Christ offers us and the changes He has made in us.

We are living in a time during which people are looking to their past to explain or excuse their failures or their present misguided behavior. We want to find someone in our past to blame for our sins and failures. Blaming someone else for where we are today keeps us from accepting personal responsibility for the choices we have made. It may make us temporarily feel better, but it rarely ever solves the problem. It simply deflects the blame.

It is true that it is hard to forget the past. I don't think it is possible to literally forget it, but it is possible to forget it in terms of not allowing it to control our present or future. If we have truly repented and turned our back on our sinful past, and accepted salvation on God's terms, then we have been forgiven. Forgetting the past is not an issue of erasing our memory so much as it is an issue of motivating us to go beyond our sordid past and not get permanently stuck in it. Anyone who makes the mistake of dwelling on the past may experience deep and significant regrets. When he looked back, Paul said he was the "foremost" of sinners (1 Timothy 1:15). Peter said, "I am a sinful man" (Luke 5:8). Isaiah said "Woe is me! For I am lost; for I am a man of unclean lips, and I dwell in the midst of a people of unclean lips" (Isaiah 6:5). "All have sinned and fall short of the glory of God" (Romans 3:23), and "none is righteous, no, not one" (Romans 3:10). The only thing that separates us—any one of us—from another is the wonderful grace and mercy of God, which we accept through obedience and trust.

Past Neglect

Sometimes as we grow older, the main things we regret are the things we did not do—the missed opportunities with our spouse, children, or good friends. If there is any value at all in regrets, it is that we regret our past sins to the extent we repent of them and move forward. We remove the regrets and replace them with the joy of our current salvation. We experience gratitude for the forgiveness of others and most of all for the forgiveness of God. We will never regret repenting of our sins and confessing our faith in Jesus Christ. We will never regret being baptized for the

CHAPTER 4

remission of our sins and being added to the Lord's church. We will never regret developing the fruit of the Spirit in our lives, becoming more like Christ every day. We will never regret the cleansing of our sins which produces a clean conscience and a more sensitive realization of what is good and bad. We will never regret following the truth and standing for the truth, for that is what sets us free from our past sins (John 8:32). We should never regret the sacrifices we make for others because we have put Christ and His will first in our lives. His life and teachings are our compass and guide.

We need to accept the fact that we have failed in the past, that we may even be somewhat dissatisfied with our present state in that we haven't become as godly as we want to be. The Christian life is a matter of growing daily in the grace and knowledge of our Lord. It is pictured by Paul as a race to be run, a race that will not end until we pass from this life and receive the crown of life. The way Paul responded to his life in our text was a mark of true spiritual maturity.

We must never get to the point where we are stuck in the past or where we think we have arrived, that we have all the answers, that we are as spiritual as we need to be because we have not reached perfection (Galatians 6:3). Paul realized that he was not perfect, and we should, too. But Paul was unwilling to give up, and he was unwilling to be deterred by his past.

So many get discouraged with their lives and drop out of the race. Our failures and successes should never cause us to do this. Paul said, "...one thing I do: forgetting what lies behind" (Philippians 3:13). I know few people who are completely successful at doing this. Most of us are pulled in many different directions and find it difficult to do this one thing—"forgetting those things which are behind." We should no longer allow our past sins to affect our present and future.

In Philippians 3:13, Paul says "straining forward." Again he uses the analogy of a runner in a race. As we near the finish line (as we get older), the runner leans forward, straining to reach the goal. Reaching out with all we have, exerting every effort to be sure we win the race and cross the finish line. Verse 14 says, "I press on toward the goal." The runner doesn't take his eye off the goal. It is always in view. Paul practiced what he preached and gave his own testimony recorded in 2 Timothy 4:6,7: "For I am already being poured out as a drink offering, and the time of my departure has come. I have fought the good fight, I have finished the race, I have kept the faith." We highly respect a person who backs up his advice with an exemplary life. Paul did just that. In verse 14, Paul says that he is running "for the prize." He is running to be able to spend forever with the Lord in heaven. Paul was willing to put up with all of the difficulties, pressures, and problems of this life so that he could lead others to Christ and win the prize at the end of the race. Thankfully, he got what he was after: First Timothy 4:8, "Henceforth there is laid up for me the crown of righteousness, which the Lord, the righteous judge, will award to me on that Day, and not only to me but also to all who have loved his appearing." Paul describes this victory, this prize, as a high calling, meaning a life above the average, a life of excellence, purity, devotion, and sacrifice. Most of the world is unwilling to try to attain these qualities. The Christian life is truly a higher calling.

From time to time I have to stop and ask myself, *How well am I running the race? Are my eyes on Jesus alone? Am I allowing the distractions of the past to get me off course?* Taking a life inventory can help us adjust our spiritual compass.

Manna from Heaven, Food For Thought

"Give justice to the weak and the fatherless; maintain the right of the afflicted and the destitute. Rescue the weak and the needy; deliver them from the hand of the wicked" (Psalm 82:3,4).

CHAPTER 4

"Above all, keep loving one another earnestly, since love covers a multitude of sins" (1 Peter 4:8).

"For this very reason, make every effort to supplement your faith with virtue, and virtue with knowledge, and knowledge with self-control, and self-control with steadfastness, and steadfastness with godliness, and godliness with brotherly affection, and brotherly affection with love. For if these qualities are yours and increasing, they keep you from being ineffective or unfruitful in the knowledge of our Lord Jesus Christ. For whoever lacks these qualities is so nearsighted that he is blind, having forgotten that he was cleansed from his former sins. Therefore, brothers, be all the more diligent to confirm your calling and election, for if you practice these qualities you will never fall" (2 Peter 1:5-10).

There are two elements involved in forgiveness. We are willing to forgive others who have wronged us, even sinned against us, because God through Jesus has forgiven us when we have wronged and sinned against Him. "For if you forgive others their trespasses, your heavenly Father will also forgive you, but if you do not forgive others their trespasses, neither will your Father forgive your trespasses" (Matthew 6:14,15). Until and unless we forgive those who ask for our forgiveness, then we will never receive forgiveness from God. Before we can adequately forget the sins and trespasses of those who may have hurt us in the past, we must be willing to forgive them. As long as we carry around bitterness, anger, hatred, and malice in our hearts, we will never find the peace that God offers each one of us. It is only by cleansing our soul and spirit through forgiveness that we are able to receive the forgiveness of God, and often the forgiveness of others, and experience the peace that passes our understanding.

Questions

1. What are some of the dangers of living in the past?
2. Discuss the necessity for Paul to forget his early past so that he could fulfill Christ's mission for him. Read and discuss Philippians 3:12-14 and 4:8,9.
3. What did Jesus mean in Luke 9:62?
4. Are we proud of all of our history? Are there things for which we need to repent and forget?
5. Discuss the blessing of God's and our fellow man's forgiveness.
6. What is the danger of using our past as an excuse for our present failures?
7. Discuss Paul's analogy in Philippians 3 of running a race and how that applies to older Christians.
8. What are the two elements involved in forgiveness?

CHAPTER 5

WE NEED ONE ANOTHER: FELLOWSHIP

No Man Is An Island

No man is an island, Entire of itself,
Every man is a piece of the continent, A part of the main.
If a clod be washed away by the sea, Europe is the less.
As well as if a promontory were.
As well as if a manor of thy friend's Or of thine own were:
Any man's death diminishes me,
Because I am involved in mankind,
And therefore never send to know for whom the bell tolls;
It tolls for thee.

John Donne

A Little Humor
Lord, how could I send a congratulations card to my friend when I meant to choose a sympathy card because her husband died? I knew they were having trouble in their marriage, but I didn't mean to take my support to that extreme. Please help her to forgive me. (Karen O'Connor)

Fellowship
Fellowship is one of those words that sounds like its meaning. It has such a pleasant sound. It invokes all kinds of images in our mind—the sharing of good as well as bad, helping one another, sympathizing with others, being there for one another, having a common philosophy of life and common goals, sharing the

CHAPTER 5

deepest feelings and emotions of life. It is a word that describes one of the most needed elements of everyone's life, and especially the lives of Christians. The reality is that we need each other. We need to be able to depend on each other, sharing our joys and sorrows. We gain strength, encouragement, and edification from being in the presence of one another.

The older we get, the more we need true fellowship. We need to be able to have someone in whom we can confide and with whom we can share common aging experiences. George Burns said that he had always been taught to respect his elders. Near the end of his life, he said that he had no one left to respect. He had outlived all of his friends. We are better able to meet the challenges of older age if we have someone with whom we can share the experience. Loneliness—being isolated, out of touch, and sometimes seemingly forgotten—is one of the major complaints of many older people. We all need a support group, and for those of us who are Christians, a major part of that support group should be the church and our families.

That is the reason that "religion that is pure and undefiled before God the Father is this: to visit orphans and widows in their affliction, and to keep oneself unstained from the world" (James 1:27). That means to be there for those who are older and have lost their spouses or those who have been orphaned. How well is the church meeting this need? We have many youth ministers, but I am aware of only a few ministers to the older segment of congregations. Yet the needs of the older are just as critical as those of the younger, and if we are a church following the example and pattern of the first-century church, we will be interested in and take care of our older members. In fact, that is one of the major reasons why deacons were appointed in the church—to meet the needs of the Grecian widows, many of whom at the time felt they were being neglected.

There are two kinds of fellowship that are essential for older

Christians. The first and most important, and prerequisite to the second, is fellowship with God. Our need and dependency on God grows as we get older. I have heard several of my older friends say recently that when they lose something, forget something, or need something, they simply pray to God because there is really nowhere else they can go for help. I think that is perfectly legitimate, to pray that God will help us find something that we need that has been lost or that He will give us peace about a particular situation that may be bothering us. We must have fellowship with God at any age to be complete.

Win Arn, a church consultant, sent questionnaires to nearly 1,000 churches, asking them the simple question: "Why does the church exist?" Of the members of the church who were surveyed, 89 percent said "the church's purpose is to take care of my family and my needs." Then he asked the same question of the ministers. Over 90 percent of the ministers surveyed said the purpose of the church was to win the world to Christ. Only 10 percent said it was to care for the needs of the members of the local churches. The ministers' attitude toward the church's purpose was opposite to that of the members. That may be one reason why there are so many churches that have lost their direction and are losing members. We must know what our purpose is—the reason for our existence—before we can move in the proper direction.

The early church knew its purpose. They were completely unified. "Now the full number of those who believed were of one heart and one soul… And with great power the apostles were giving their testimony to the resurrection of the Lord Jesus, and great grace was upon them all" (Acts 4:32, 33). The early church had been called to a life of service and sacrifice, and their desire was to share what they had found with others.

The Bible often speaks of the church as a family: brothers and sisters in Christ; God, the Father, and Jesus, the elder brother. These early Christians had shared a common spiritual birth. They

CHAPTER 5

were born into the kingdom of God, the family of God, by water and by the Spirit. The blood of Jesus Christ had washed away their sins and they were a part of God's family, sharing everything together as any family would. They shared their possessions with one another when needs arose, and they certainly were there to comfort and encourage one another in times of difficulty. They rejoiced together in times of victory.

These early Christians were from all nations who had come together to observe Pentecost. Many were far from home and the extended stay placed financial and physical difficulties on them. But because of the local Christians sharing what they had, all needs were adequately met. In Acts 2:41, the passage ends with "those who received his word were baptized, and there were added that day about three thousand souls."

The chapter goes on to tell us how they merged their lives together for a common cause:

> And they devoted themselves to the apostles' teaching and the fellowship, to the breaking of bread and the prayers. And awe came upon every soul, and many wonders and signs were being done through the apostles. And all who believed were together and had all things in common. And they were selling their possessions and belongings and distributing the proceeds to all, as any had need. And day by day, attending the temple together and breaking bread in their homes, they received their food with glad and generous hearts, praising God and having favor with all the people. And the Lord added to their number day by day those who were being saved (Acts 2:42-47).

Every aspect of the Christian's life is a part of fellowship. Preaching, singing, giving, and observing the Lord's communion are all a part of fellowship. Everything we do as God's people should include at least some element of fellowship. I wonder if this is our attitude toward the church today. Is this the way we view the Lord's church in the 21st century? We must resist comfortable Christianity. Our culture has often corrupted the biblical concept of the church. Some churches have lost the vision of why we exist as God's church. If Jesus visited many of our churches today, I wonder if He would think we have in so many ways corrupted the concept of the church and are often preaching a prosperity version of Christianity. This version is individually centered, rather than Christ-centered, with an atmosphere of little or no sacrifice and, in most instances, no inconvenience on the Christian's part. Many churches have eliminated the concept of service and have replaced it with, "Meet my physical and emotional needs. That's enough." Some churches have quit preaching about the true God and have substituted a kind of Santa Claus God who will grant our every wish and give us whatever we want. For the sake of larger crowds and larger budgets, we have watered down the gospel message to a social gospel and the church in many instances to a social club. Many preachers are simply secular psychologists, life coaches, or cheerleaders who rarely if ever preach the good news of the Savior—the one who came to give forgiveness of our sins and create in us a higher calling and as much as possible a sin-free life. We need ministers who tell us the truth about what is wrong with us and what it will take to fix what is wrong. It seems that contemporary Christianity has lost the purpose of the church, in part because people want to hear that they are okay, and that in some way, the church will give them what they want. This attitude certainly does not encourage us to a sacrificial life and a life of helping meet the needs of others. In fact, the opposite is true. It becomes narcissistic and devoid of a true understanding of the meaning of the word *fellowship*.

One other note: The internet or telephone can never replace face-to-face, one-on-one Christian fellowship. In fact, if anything, our modern means of communication may have created a nameless, faceless type of inferior fellowship. Theologian Carl Trueman writes, "The language of friendship is hijacked and cheapened by internet social networks." He further says, "The

CHAPTER 5

language of Facebook both reflects and encourages childishness," and has, he writes, "become something of a textually transmitted disease." The reason he uses the word *childish* is because much of our modern communication is self-centered and an indication of the "me and my" generation. He points out "the relationships are developed by the disembodied world of the web and create human amoebas substituting in a bizarre non-world that involves no risk to themselves, no giving of themselves to others, no true vulnerability, no commitment, no sacrifice, no real meaning, and no value." This may be a little overstated. The internet can be a wonderful tool for communication, but it can never take the place of human contact, one-on-one, looking each other in the eye, seeing the expressions on the face and reaching out with the hand of friendship and fellowship.

Nature's Way of Caring for the Elderly

In a wolf pack, the first three wolves are the old or sick. They set the pace to the entire pack. If it were the other way around, they would be left behind, losing contact with the pack. In case of an ambush, they would be sacrificed. Next in line are five strong ones, the front line. In the center are the rest of the pack members, that are then followed by the five strongest. The last one is the lone wolf, the alpha. He controls everything from the rear. In that position, he can see everything and decide the direction. He sees all of the pack. The pack moves according to the elders' pace, helping and watching one another.

Fellowship With God First

Without a true relationship with God the Father and Jesus our Savior, there can be no effective fellowship among members of His kingdom church. We share in the glorious new birth, being born again as babes in Christ. That shared redemptive process is essential to each individual member's experiencing real fellowship. On the day of Pentecost when the church was established and 3,000 people were baptized into Christ, becoming true Christians, they immediately understood the meaning of the family of God and what is required to be true brothers and sisters in this family. That shared togetherness is essential in our fellowship. Becoming a Christian allows us the understanding and privilege of being members of God's family in which we have a continual and meaningful shared fellowship. As brothers and sisters, we are there for one another at all times, helping meet each others' needs and encouraging one another to be faithful to the end.

Clearly the basis for fellowship is salvation. One purpose of the gospel is to produce a fellowship with other believers, with God, with Christ, and with the Holy Spirit. If we are truly in Christ, then we have that fellowship. Fellowship has always involved more serving and less receiving. As older Christians, we need more than ever to have assurance about our salvation—not that we are perfect, but we strive for perfection, and that we honestly believe that we have done everything Jesus has asked us to do to become a child of God and that we are seeking to serve Him in every way we can.

Christian friends want to be together. We want to be together and enjoy sweet and beautiful friendship and fellowship here and hereafter. As Christians, we share so much and have received so many common promises and blessings. Among these promises are those from God through Jesus Christ, which allow us to know that, though we may be forsaken and abandoned by everyone else, we still have the essential fellowship of God through Christ.

CHAPTER 5

We are assured of that fellowship in Scripture: "I am with you always" (Matthew 28:20); "I will never leave you nor forsake you" (Hebrews 13:5); and Jesus is preparing a place for us in heaven "so we will always be with the Lord" (1 Thessalonians 4:17). Heaven will more than compensate for the trials, tribulations, and loneliness we experience here. First and foremost, we have a friend in Jesus, and we also have fellowship with brothers and sisters as we travel the road of life.

Some older people get to the point where they are ready to go home and be with God. They know they must live their life to the end, but if given the choice, they would rather go home. One of the Scripture passages that best describes our desire for home is in Philippians: "For me to live is Christ, and to die is gain. If I am to live in the flesh, that means fruitful labor for me. Yet which I shall choose I cannot tell. I am hard pressed between the two. My desire is to depart and be with Christ, for that is far better" (1:21-23).

A Modern Example

Dietrich Bonhoeffer, a German theologian and author, was confined to a prison camp in Flossenburg, Germany because of his Christian beliefs. Being isolated from Christian companions while in prison, as many elderly are isolated in independent living homes or nursing homes, he sought a purpose for his being there. As a result, he became a counselor and spiritual advisor to many other prisoners in that concentration camp. He also wrote often about fellowship—fellowship with God and with other Christians. This is much like Paul as he was imprisoned in Rome, isolated from those to whom he had been closest in his ministry. When we are isolated and alone, desperately in need of fellowship, we need to reach out to friends, family, and especially to our Christian brothers and sisters to help us through these lonely times. Bonhoeffer was hanged on April 9, 1945, only a few days before the Americans liberated that concentration camp. But his martyrdom drew attention to many of his writings, including those entitled *Letters and Papers from Prison*. He never gave up his faith or questioned his circumstances, and he used his talents and abilities to the very end and to the glory of God. So must we!

None of us knows what lies ahead. The world is in such turmoil and confusion. It may be before our lives end that we will be isolated and separated from those who mean the most to us. It is then that we cling to our Savior and Lord and to His comforting words, "I will be with you always, even to the end."

Food For Thought:

"Whoever loves transgression loves strife; he who makes his door high seeks destruction" (Proverbs 17:19).

"Iron sharpens iron, and one man sharpens another" (Proverbs 27:17).

"A friend loves at all times, and a brother is born for adversity" (Proverbs 17:17).

"Faithful are the wounds of a friend; profuse are the kisses of an enemy" (Proverbs 27:6).

"I am a companion of all who fear you, of those who keep your precepts" (Psalm 119:63).

"Then Jonathan made a covenant with David, because he loved him as his own soul" (1 Samuel 18:3).

"Then Jonathan said to David, 'Whatever you say, I will do for you'" (1 Samuel 20:4).

"Rejoice with those who rejoice, weep with those who weep" (Romans 12:15).

"Greater love has no one than this, that someone lay down his life for his friends" (John 15:13).

"Whoever walks with the wise will become wise, but the companion of fools will suffer harm" (Proverbs 13:20).

CHAPTER 5

"Religion that is pure and undefiled before God the Father is this: to visit orphans and widows in their affliction, and to keep oneself unstained from the world" (James 1:27).

Questions

1. Discuss the meaning of the word *fellowship*.
2. Why is true fellowship so essential as we get older?
3. Discuss James 1:27 ("pure religion").
4. Are most widows and widowers also orphans in that their parents have usually passed? Can you be an older orphan?
5. How well is the church meeting its responsibility toward its aging population?
6. What are the two essential kinds of fellowship for older Christians?
7. Discuss how fellowship was essential in the early church.
8. Discuss the importance of the family of God. How do we become brothers and sisters in Christ?
9. What are the many ways we can share fellowship with one another?
10. How is modern technology affecting personal fellowship?
11. Why do Christian friends want to be together, spending time with each other?
12. Do you know people who have expressed a desire to go home and be with God in heaven, experiencing the most important fellowship of all—that with God the Father and Son?

CHAPTER 6

WORRY – ANXIETY

A Little Humor

Tom Moore, in an article entitled "Overcoming Worry," wrote, "It seems that worry is the watchword of our world today. No job, we worry, then we get a job and we worry. No money, we worry, then we earn money and still worry. Sick, and we worry, then we get well and we still worry." As much as anything else, worry is a habit we need to break. We need to do what God asks us to do. Read Matthew 6:33-34: "But seek first the kingdom of God and his righteousness, and all these things will be added to you..." (These things He refers to here are the necessities and essentials of life which we will be discussing—food, shelter, clothing.) "Do not be anxious about tomorrow, for tomorrow will be anxious for itself. Sufficient for the day is its own trouble."

Do Not Fear

Our fears, worries, and anxieties often increase as we age, even though they may take a little different twist than when we were younger. When young, we are full of hope and ambition, with our future ahead of us. We wonder if we will succeed or fail. That brings some apprehension. But most of us, when we are young, are strong and capable of meeting the challenges to support ourselves and our families. We have been fortunate to live in a country where if disaster strikes and we are unable to work for a while, we have a governmental safety net that allows us time to recover, re-focus, re-educate ourselves, and get back into the working society. Even those who are younger with permanent disabilities are able

CHAPTER 6

to at least receive assistance through Social Security Insurance and disability. This is certainly not an ideal situation, but it is an alternative that has sustained millions of people with one type of disability or another.

When we are older, we are on the other end of life's spectrum. I think the primary difference between young and old is, as older people, we have experience and a life full of proof of God's providential care for us. As an older person myself, I do not place my faith at this point in government to bail me out if I have a problem. More than ever, it is in God, knowing that He will not forsake His children.

During our lifetimes, we wonder if we will get to the point where we won't have enough food, enough clothing, or adequate shelter. But as we become senior citizens and look back on life, we see that God has always been there for us. He may not have given us exactly what we wanted in the way we wanted it, but most of us have never been truly hungry for any period of time. In fact, many people who go hungry today do so because they simply do not want or like the nourishment that may be available to them or because they are on a diet caused by overeating. Most of us have always had adequate food, clothing, and shelter.

Our homes may not have been mansions, but they were enough to keep us comfortable, full, and warm. Our clothes may not have had designer labels, but they kept us warm, comfortable, and modest.

The promise of God to provide for His people and take care of the essentials of life is nowhere more clearly presented than in Matthew 6. Those of us who have lived to our senior years look back on the life where God has kept His promises better than we have probably kept our promises to seek Him first, and all of these things will be added to us. His grace and mercy have abounded in meeting all our needs.

Though we may often feel sorry for ourselves today for our

plight, we have it so much better than our grandparents and great-grandparents, and even most people in the world today. My grandmother Swaim died at age 96. Until she was 90, she lived in a house (actually a country shack) where she had raised nine children and been widowed for more than 30 years. Her house had no running water. Instead, she drew water with a bucket from an outside well. The outhouse was 30 yards from the house. Wood-burning, pot-bellied stoves provided the home's only heat. The only way to cook was on a wood-burning stove. She did not have electricity until a few years before she moved, and that only consisted of a wire on a pole running from the dirt road in front of her house to the house, and more wires stapled to the ceiling of her small living area. This part of the house also served as her quilting area, with the quilts pulled up to the ceiling in the evening and let down during the day. She had one dangling wire with a bulb in it in that room, another in the bedroom, and one more in the kitchen. That was the extent of her electricity. My father and his brothers, who lived far away from her, would make sure that she had plenty of wood cut and stacked on the porch where she could get to it easily in the winter. She had no Social Security. Isolated in the Arkansas countryside, she had never contributed to Social Security and did not depend on anyone other than herself, what meager savings she had been able to accumulate, and the faithful generosity of her children. Her wants and needs were simple, and her faith was as solid as the strongest steel. She would say, when asked if she needed anything, "I have everything I desire." And she did, because her desires were so few—basically, just the fulfillment of her needs.

Our expectations are often unrealistic, and if we have to settle for just the basic needs of food, shelter, and clothing, we may feel God has failed us. But actually, that is all we need. As we grow older, our wants and needs often decrease to the basic, simplest,

CHAPTER 6

and often happiest period of our lives. Others' expectations of us are low, and there is little or no pressure to show off with superfluous or gaudy opulence. Many of the things that Donna and I have acquired over the years no longer mean as much to us as we grow older. I have been an avid hunter all of my life, and trophies from around the world are scattered from one end of our house to the other. These no longer mean as much to me, and I now fully understand the meaning of "laying down our trophies at Jesus' feet." The only things that really matter at this point in my life are living as faithful a life as possible, because I know the Christian life in every way is the best life to be lived, and looking forward to spending forever with our Creator and Savior and all of those faithful followers of the past.

Jesus Says

Jesus puts our life here on earth in crystal clear perspective in Matthew 6 where He spotlights what is and isn't important, and where He tells us how to receive the providential care of God in every stage of life.

> Therefore I tell you, do not be anxious about your life, what you will eat or what you will drink, nor about your body, what you will put on. Is not life more than food, and the body more than clothing? Look at the birds of the air: they neither sow nor reap nor gather into barns, and yet your heavenly Father feeds them. Are you not of more value than they? And which of you by being anxious can add a single hour to his span of life? And why are you anxious about clothing? Consider the lilies of the field, how they grow: they neither toil nor spin, yet I tell you, even Solomon in all his glory was not arrayed like one of these. But if God so clothes the grass of the field, which today is alive and tomorrow is thrown into the oven, will he not much more clothe you, O you of little faith? Therefore do not be anxious, saying, "What shall we eat?" or "What shall we drink?" or "What shall we wear?" For the Gentiles seek after all these things, and your heavenly Father knows that you need them all. But seek

first the kingdom of God and his righteousness, and all these things will be added to you (Matthew 6:25-34).

This text gives us the secret keys to eliminating worry and anxiety from our life. It is a text for every person, regardless of age. It clearly teaches us how to overcome the temptation to fear and be anxious. The Bible teaches that worry is the opposite of faith. For the Christian, worry indicates that we may not trust God. Jesus makes it clear in this passage that anyone can understand how God will provide for us when we are seeking first His kingdom and loving Him first. The text talks about all of our basic needs—food, clothing, shelter. God's care is illustrated by the birds and the flowers. Did you know that there are more than 8,000 species of birds and, according to God's Word, He feeds them all. Some scientists go so far as to estimate the number of species to be much higher, perhaps billions of birds, and God cares for all of them.

Jesus teaches us here that we are to stop worrying about survival. Survival, for the faithful Christian, is not a problem. We need to put away the anxiety we have over daily necessities. How many times have you gone hungry? How many times have you been without clothing? How many times have you been without shelter? In comparison to your life, your answer is likely few, if any. The flowers of the field bloom beautifully every year. In fact, their color, beauty, and radiance surpass that of King Solomon in all his glory. If you are a faithful Christian, you are the object of God's love, attention, and care.

God Knows

God knows exactly what we need. While we spend our time worrying and wringing our hands, God is working, preparing, and providing for our needs. We don't need to be anxious about tomorrow. Worry and anxiety never give us strength for tomorrow. Worry and anxiety drain our strength for today. If you can get

CHAPTER 6

through today, God will be there tomorrow to continue His care. These two illustrations in verses 26 and 30 show God's care for His creation. God did not mean for His children to worry about the necessities of life. There are more than 100 disorders and diseases that can be directly attributed to unnecessary worry. When we worry, we get all kinds of aches and pains, such as headaches, backaches, and stomachaches. Every day, Americans consume 15 tons of aspirin, much of it to relieve the aches and pains associated with worry.

Worry never accomplishes anything worthwhile. Jesus indicates that in Matthew 6:27 when He says, "And which of you by being anxious can add a single hour to his span of life?" Worry may shorten your life but it rarely, if ever, will lengthen it. And the really sad thing, according to verse 30, is that since God takes care of the flowers and the birds, will He not much more clothe and take care of us? And then He adds, "O you of little faith." Since God knows how to take care of the birds of the air and the flowers of the field, He certainly knows how to take care of His children. Read Psalm 145:15: "The eyes of all look to you, and you give them their food in due season." Remember God's care for Israel in the wilderness. Worrying about the necessities of life is what people who do not believe in God do. They realize they are strictly on their own, and get no help from the Creator. For God's children to worry shows a definite lack of faith in His promises. Matthew 6:31, 32 reminds us: "Therefore do not be anxious, saying, 'What shall we eat?' or 'What shall we drink?' or 'What shall we wear?' For the Gentiles seek after all these things." As God's children, we have His promise that He will provide the necessities of life for us.

I know what may be in the back of your mind. *Yes, I know that's what the Bible says, but I'm worried that I may outlive my money.* Or *I'm worried that Social Security may go bankrupt.* Or *I'm worried that the economy may collapse.* Or *I'm worried that my children either will not or cannot take care of me should I need their help.* Stop worrying. No matter what happens, you have God's word that He will provide for you. He simply asks you to love Him, to love and care about (and for) your fellow man, and to be faithful till death.

Paul, who earned his way everywhere he went, said, "Do not be anxious about anything, but in everything by prayer and supplication with thanksgiving let your requests be made known to God. And the peace of God, which surpasses all understanding, will guard your hearts and your minds in Christ Jesus" (Philippians 4:6, 7).

The following verses from 2 Corinthians 4 have always helped me when I've experienced difficult times. Paul begins in the first two verses by saying, "We do not lose heart…we have renounced disgraceful, underhanded ways. We refuse to practice cunning or to tamper with God's word, but by the open statement of the truth we would commend ourselves to everyone's conscience in the sight of God." So first, we do everything possible to get our lives right with God as much as we can. Then in verse 3 Paul focuses on the gospel, which is the good news of Jesus Christ. We need to keep our priorities in order. The gospel, the good news, is where we need to place our confidence, trust, and faith. Paul points out that even if it is veiled to those who are lost and have been blinded by unbelief, there is hope because the light of the Christian's faith shines in darkness (verse 6). That hope in Jesus Christ allows us to overcome many of the obstacles and problems of life.

Paul further shows us that the treasure of the gospel is kept in earthen vessels, or jars of clay: "We are afflicted in every way, but not crushed; perplexed, but not driven to despair; persecuted, but not forsaken; struck down, but not destroyed; always carrying in the body the death of Jesus, so that the life of Jesus may also be manifested in our bodies" (verses 8-10). It is important

CHAPTER 6

to remember that Paul was not writing this information while sitting on the beach in a lounge chair, sipping lemonade. He was not taking a vacation and simply filling his spare time by writing. Paul never had the luxury of sitting in a recliner and enjoying the good life. Rather, his life was one of constant peril, sacrificial work, and dangerous circumstances—imprisonment, shipwrecks, facing robbers, and the Jews of his own nationality who opposed him. He was a man who knew what difficult, hard circumstances were. Yet, in light of all the problems of his life, he was able to keep a good attitude and to maintain his faith in God through Jesus Christ, which always sustained him in every difficult situation as faith will sustain us, too.

In 2 Corinthians 4:4, Paul tells us not to lose heart and then spends the rest of the chapter telling us why we are not to lose heart. As older Christians, it is easy to become discouraged, worried, and anxious. But if God is with us, and we are with God, who can be against us? The love and mercy of God to some people is veiled by money, power, prestige, lust, and greed. Many of these people will never be able to see the love, mercy, and grace of God through Jesus. Because God has entrusted His Word to us and His grace, we are able to overcome any and all obstacles.

There is confidence in Paul's words. In verse 13, he writes, "I believed..." and "I spoke..." We also believe, and so we speak, having experienced the blessings of God and known His forgiveness and grace. We can't help but tell others about His wonderful care, even in the most desperate of situations, and share with others the grace that can be extended to more and more people as we are told in verse 15. "So we do not lose heart. Though our outer self is wasting away, our inner self is being renewed day by day. For this light momentary affliction is preparing for us an eternal weight of glory beyond all comparison, as we look not to the things that are seen but to the things that are unseen. For the things that are seen are transient, but the things that are unseen are eternal" (2 Corinthians 4:16-18, ESV). What we experience here on this earth—all of the difficulties, problems, anxieties, doubts, fears, worry, pain, suffering, and sorrow—all of what Paul calls here "this light momentary affliction" is preparing us an eternal weight of glory beyond all comparison. In verse 18 he encourages us to look at the unseen things, not the things that are temporary or transient, but the things that are unseen and eternal. He wants us to focus on heaven. If we do this, then first we will be able to overcome our worries, doubts, fears, and anxieties, and we will be able to help others with their difficult situations. Finally, we will have the faith and the hope of an eternal home with God.

To summarize: (1) Paul experienced many difficulties and problems as do we. (2) The gospel, the good news of Jesus Christ, was enough to encourage and help Paul overcome all of his problems. That same gospel good news is our encouragement as well. (3) We believe and overcome and then speak as we are encouraged in verse 13. Verse 4 tells us that we must not lose heart. We do not give up, nor do we give in. Instead, we tell others about God's grace and mercy which has seen us through all of our difficult times and always provided for us. "God's spirit renews us day by day." (4) We know that whatever problems we experience do not compare with God's blessings of heaven. Yes, we fail and fall and suffer here on earth, but the faithfulness of His children will be more than compensated for by the blessings of heaven. The following passages explain it well.

> "Are they servants of Christ? I am a better one—I am talking like a madman—with far greater labors, far more imprisonments, with countless beatings, and often near death. Five times I received at the hands of the Jew the forty lashes less one. Three times I was beaten with rods. Once I was stoned. Three times I was shipwrecked; a night and a day I was adrift at sea; on frequent journeys, in danger from rivers, danger from robbers, danger from my own people, danger from Gentiles, danger in

CHAPTER 6

the city, danger in the wilderness, danger at sea, danger from false brothers; in toil and hardship, through many a sleepless night, in hunger and thirst, often without food, in cold and exposure. And, apart from other things, there is the daily pressure on me of my anxiety for all the churches. Who is weak, and I am not weak? Who is made to fall, and I am not indignant?" (2 Corinthians 11:23-29).

"Not that I am speaking of being in need, for I have learned in whatever situation I am to be content. I know how to be brought low, and I know how to abound. In any and every circumstance, I have learned the secret of facing plenty and hunger, abundance and need. I can do all things through him who strengthens me" (Philippians 4:11-13).

"Who shall separate us from the love of Christ? Shall tribulation, or distress, or persecution, or famine, or nakedness, or danger, or sword?...No, in all these things we are more than conquerors through him who loved us. For I am sure that neither death nor life, nor angels nor rulers, nor things present nor things to come, nor powers, nor height nor depth, nor anything else in all creation, will be able to separate us from the love of God in Christ Jesus our Lord" (Romans 8:35, 37-39).

In Matthew 10:9-11, Jesus said to depend on God and His faithful servants. Just let God know about your fears, worries, doubts, and anxieties. Turn them over to Him, and be assured that He will provide for you and meet all of your needs. "And my God will supply every need of yours according to his riches in glory in Christ Jesus" (Philippians 4:19). Matthew 11:28, 29 says, "Come to me, all who labor and are heavy laden, and I will give you rest. Take my yoke upon you, and learn from me, for I am gentle and lowly in heart, and you will find rest for your souls." STOP WORRYING! God is here to help you with all of your needs. He is listening to your prayers. He is on the job. That's why you can say with confidence, "I will trust God during all of my trying times. He knows what I am going through. He has never and will never leave or forsake me. He has a plan for my life, to the very end, and He will provide for me and my necessities until my last breath."

The Bible Tells It Like It Is

Nowhere in the Bible does it ever attempt to downplay our problems and difficulties. In fact, it plainly tells us that we will have problems, difficulties, pain, suffering, and sorrow as long as we live upon the earth. Note the following verses:

"Man who is born of a woman is few of days and full of trouble." (Job 14:1).

"I have said these things to you, that in me you may have peace. In the world you will have tribulation. But take heart; I have overcome the world" (John 16:33).

"For all his days are full of sorrow, and his work is a vexation. Even in the night his heart does not rest. This also is vanity." (Ecclesiastes 2:23).

All of these Scriptures testify to the fact that sin has left us with a legacy of pain, suffering, and sorrow, and we will have to do battle with these every day.

But God says, "Don't worry about these problems." I like the way it was put in the previous verse. "Don't be careful for anything. Don't worry about anything." Worry is a troubled state of mind, which results from concerns about current or potential difficulties. It actually comes from an old English word which means "to strangle," and it referred to the way predators would kill sheep by biting them on the neck and strangling them to death. This is what worry does to us. It puts a stranglehold on us both physically and spiritually. Worry can literally choke the life out of us. Faith and prayer are God's antidotes for worry. God wants us to pray passionately about the things that concern us. "Therefore, confess your sins to one another and pray for one another, that you may be healed. The prayer of a righteous person has great

CHAPTER 6

power as it is working" (James 5:16). "In the days of his flesh, Jesus offered up prayers and supplications, with loud cries and tears, to him who was able to save him from death, and he was heard because of his reverence" (Hebrews 5:7). "I appeal to you, brothers, by our Lord Jesus Christ and by the love of the Spirit, to strive together with me in your prayers to God on my behalf" (Romans 15:30). When the child of God humbly approaches the throne of God through prayer, praise, and the concerns of their heart, God hears and responds.

As we end our prayers, we are told that we should give thanks for what God has already done for all the provisions of life, for the fact that we have received so much more than we deserve in terms of our blessings, and thanksgiving for the realization that God is with us always. He hears and answers our prayers; He gives us what we need when we need it. We should be a thankful people. "Giving thanks always and for everything to God the Father in the name of our Lord Jesus Christ" (Ephesians 5:20). "And whatever you do, in word or deed, do everything in the name of the Lord Jesus, giving thanks to God the Father through him" (Colossians 3:17). We owe every good gift and blessing to God. After we have done this, we should understand the meaning of the words "a peace that passes all understanding" (See Philippians 4:6, 7). Knowing that God is in control, that He knows what is best, and that He has promised to provide for our necessities brings us a peace and a consolation that can come from no other source.

Jesus tells us "Do not be anxious about tomorrow, for tomorrow will be anxious for itself. Sufficient for the day is its own trouble" (Matthew 6:34). Don't worry about the future, for we are in the hands of God who controls the future. Doing what we can to provide for tomorrow is a good thing, but worrying about tomorrow is a sin. God provides the strength one day at a time. He gives us what we need and doesn't slow us down or encumber us with what is unnecessary. "Jesus Christ is the same yesterday and today and forever" (Hebrews 13:8). He will be doing the same things to protect us tomorrow as He has done today and as He did yesterday. His love and care gently surround and comfort us.

Questions

1. Why do you think that as we grow older, our fears, worries, and anxieties often increase?
2. Read and discuss Matthew 6:34. How does this apply to each of us as we grow older?
3. Do we as Christians need to worry about food, clothing, shelter, or any of the essentials of life? Discuss believing the promises of God as much as the commands of God.
4. Are our lives today better in a material sense than those of our grandparents? How?
5. How can our expectations often be unrealistic and sometimes unappreciative of what God has done for us?
6. What are your major worries and anxieties?
7. Read and discuss Matthew 6:25-34. Do you truly believe God knows exactly what we need and will provide for all of our true needs?
8. Do worry and anxiety directly affect us physically, mentally, and spiritually?
9. Does worry ever accomplish anything worthwhile (Matthew 6:27)?
10. Read and discuss Matthew 6:31, 32. How does that apply to our concerns and worries today?
11. Read and discuss Philippians 4:6, 7.
12. Discuss the importance of gratitude for what we have.

CHAPTER 7

BECOMING AN ENCOURAGER

A Little Humor

A frugal widow goes to the newspaper to take out an obituary for her late husband. "How much?" she asks the fellow behind the counter.

"One dollar per word," he says.
She says, "Make it 'MacGregor died.'"
"It's a five-word minimum."
She nearly faints but collects herself.
"Very well, make it 'MacGregor died. Volvo for sale.'"

(humorist Christopher Buckley)

Darling, you've always been with me on life's long,
bumpy ride. Through sickness, hair loss, bankruptcy,
You've been here by my side.
My heart attack and the house burning down,
That night the lightning struck,
And liver cancer—and now suddenly,
I'm starting to think that you're bad luck.

(comedian Erica Rhodes)

Growing old is a goal to which most of us aspire. We should never regret growing old, because it is a privilege denied to many. Yet as most people approach older age, they do so with apprehension, because in some ways it is a frightening experience. Our bodies are weakening. We become susceptible to various

CHAPTER 7

kinds of diseases. We decline in strength. As we retire, we may be overwhelmed with a sense of uselessness. We are at the age where many of our friends and loved ones are dying, and there is a realization of our own mortality. Yet, despite all of the negatives, growing older can and should be a positive experience. All too often, however, these are the ways of describing the aging process from those with whom I counsel or interview:

- Hurting
- Sad
- Desperate
- Alone
- Rejected
- Ignored

- Forsaken by friends
- Forgotten
- Afraid
- Very sick
- No one available to help me
- No one to be a good friend

That is a negative description of the aging process, yet these are feelings that many experience. What we really need is a compassionate church full of those willing to be an encouragement and encourager. We all need to be lifted up from time-to-time. Paul often spoke of those who had encouraged him. I think as we approach older age, we expect the problems that come to us physically, mentally, and maybe even emotionally. But most are unprepared for the fear, worry, loneliness, feelings of panic, being self-absorbed with our own problems, and feeling unappreciated. All of these are frightening experiences. How wonderful it is when there are those in the body of Christ who reach out to those in need with a helping hand and a kind word, lifting them up and helping them through difficult times.

Often in the beginning and ending of the letters written by Paul, he acknowledges those who were instrumental in encouraging him in his work, emphasizing the fact that we need one another and depend on encouragement from those around us. In Romans 16:3-16, Paul identifies several people who have been supporters and encouragers. In verses 3-5, he talks about Aquila and Priscilla, who on numerous occasions were helpful and encouraging to Paul. Concerning this couple, he says they "risked their necks for my life" (Romans 16:4). I wonder how many friends we have who would actually risk their lives for us? Just as they had helped Paul establish the church in Corinth, verse 5 indicates they also had a major part in the church at Rome. Paul also singles out Epaenetus, the "first convert to Christ in Asia" (Romans 16:5). In some way or the other, he had been a true encourager to Paul. I suppose each of us could look back on our own lives and remember people who are not well-known, but who at one time or another were an encouragement, uplifting and strengthening us.

Mary is the next person mentioned in Romans 16:6. Though we are not sure which Mary this was, we do know she "worked hard." In verse 7, Paul speaks of Andronicus and Junia, who may have been kinsmen or, at the very least, countrymen, of Paul. (The same word here translated "kinsmen" can also be used to identify those from the same country.) These two are called "fellow prisoners," and also "well known to the apostles." Verse 8 mentions Ampliatus. He was a slave, but an encourager to Paul. Verse 9 mentions Urbanus and Stachys, whose claim to fame was that they were there for Paul when he needed them. In verse 10, he speaks of Apelles, who had been tested and found "approved in Christ." Verse 11 tells of Herodion and Narcissus. Some believe Narcissus was a high official to Emperor Claudius. In verse 12 we read of Tryphaena and Tryphosa (no doubt twin sisters—their names translate to "delicate" and "dainty"), along with Persis "who has worked hard in the Lord." All these were faithful encouragers to Paul and a great blessing in his ministry. In verse 13 there is Rufus, who may be the son of Simon of Cyrene mentioned in Mark 15:21. Verse 15 tells us of Philologus and Julia (probably a married couple), Nereus and his sister, and Olympas. In verse 16, Paul instructs them to "greet one another with a holy kiss," indicating deep affection and friendship. All

CHAPTER 7

of these mentioned here in one way or another were an encouragement to Paul. His spirits must have been lifted each time he was in their presence, being encouraged by their words, their sacrificial acts of kindness, and by the common strong faith they shared together.

In the biblical account of history, these people are only footnotes, yet their acts of encouragement and kindness should be an inspiration to each one of us to "bear one another's burdens" and help one another through the difficult times of our lives.

The Encourager

We could not do justice to the subject of encouragement without looking at Barnabas. "Thus Joseph, who was also called by the apostles Barnabas (which means son of encouragement), a Levite, a native of Cyprus, sold a field that belonged to him and brought the money and laid it at the apostles' feet" (Acts 4:36, 37). At first Barnabas is introduced to us by his parent-given name of Joseph. But we quickly see why the apostles gave him the name Barnabas, which means "son of encouragement." This new name indicated the kind of person he was. He was a person who brought out the best in other people. He helped meet their needs, and when others may have criticized someone, he found the good in them and encouraged them to pursue a more positive direction. He had the special gift of recognizing when people were in need.

After Saul's experience on the Damascus road, he eventually returned to Jerusalem. As he began to preach and teach, trying to win people to Jesus, there was an element who did not trust him. They felt that he was still a persecutor of "the Way," trying to infiltrate the church so that he could gain information to persecute them. After all, he was on his way to Damascus to imprison Christians. Yet at a time when Paul needed someone to speak for him, to believe in him and the sincerity of his conversion, it was Barnabas who reached out to him. "But Barnabas took him and brought him to the apostles and declared to them how on the road he had seen the Lord, who spoke to him, and how at Damascus he had preached boldly in the name of Jesus" (Acts 9:27). Barnabas encouraged Paul to become a part of the Jerusalem church. It was also Barnabas who was selected by the Jerusalem church to go to Antioch and investigate rumors that there were problems in the church there. When he reached Antioch and observed the faith of those Christians he said, "he was glad" (Acts 11:23), again displaying this integral part of his personality to encourage people.

Unfortunately brethren do not always get along or see eye-to-eye on various aspects of how to deal with difficult situations. On the first missionary journey, Paul and Barnabas were successful in establishing many churches. They had taken with them a young Christian named John Mark. But for one reason or another, John Mark became discouraged and turned back. This, no doubt, placed an added burden on Paul and Barnabas. When they began preparation for their second missionary journey, Barnabas wanted to take John Mark, but Paul vehemently refused. "Now Barnabas wanted to take with them John called Mark. But Paul thought best not to take with them one who had withdrawn from them in Pamphylia and had not gone with them to the work" (Acts 15:37, 38). As a result, Paul and Barnabas had a disagreement, which ended with the two of them going in different directions. Paul refused to allow John Mark a second chance, but Barnabas, being the encourager he was, believed John Mark deserved another chance. So Paul and Silas went one way, and Barnabas and John Mark went another—and the work they accomplished was doubled! "And there arose a sharp disagreement, so that they separated from each other. Barnabas took Mark, with him and sailed away to Cyprus, but Paul chose Silas and departed, having been commended by the brothers to the grace of the Lord" (Acts 15:39, 40).

CHAPTER 7

There is no doubt that Barnabas's confidence in John Mark to be a part of the second missionary journey was a major factor in his faithfulness to the Lord and to the church for the rest of his life. If you open your Bible to the New Testament, you will find Matthew and then Mark. That Mark is the same Mark, John Mark, who was encouraged to service and given a second chance by Barnabas the encourager.

What We Need

In the church today, one of our greatest needs is for men and women to encourage those who are struggling. To me there is no greater need. We have plenty of amateur critics and fault-finders. What we seriously lack are encouragers and uplifters. To me, one of the most gratifying passages of Scripture is found in 2 Timothy 4:11, where Paul is in a Roman prison at the end of his life. He writes to Timothy and says, "Luke alone is with me. Get Mark and bring him with you, for he is very useful to me for ministry." That Mark of whom Paul speaks is the same Mark he refused to allow to go on the second missionary journey. But because of Barnabas's belief in Mark and willingness to encourage him and give him a second chance, Mark proves worthy. Paul acknowledges that worthiness by saying Mark is "very useful to me for ministry." Who knows what the result of our encouragement will be in the life of someone who, because of our words of love, compassion, forgiveness and encouragement, may go on to be a great servant in the kingdom of God.

Young or old, all of us need occasional encouragement. We need to encourage those who are in pain or suffering whether that pain is physical, mental, or spiritual. Having practiced as a psychotherapist for 30 years, I have a unique insight into the pain and heartache people suffer. I could not count the times when someone would come into our session excited, uplifted, and encouraged because someone had taken the time to listen to them, to give them a positive message of hope, and to tell them they were praying for them.

So many events in our life can cause us deep, deep pain. Whether it's the physical pain of illness or accident or the emotional pain of the loss of a loved one, a divorce, or sickness of a child, every one of us needs words of encouragement. Loneliness is one of the major curses of older age. More than 20 million Americans live by themselves. I am amazed at the extent to which people go to be acknowledged and recognized. It is sad that people so often resort to compromising, using illegitimate methods of attention-seeking, just to kind of wave a white flag saying, "I am still here—still alive. Someone notice me. I need someone to talk with." Those who are true encouragers have a sixth sense, a kind of antenna, that causes them to zero in on those people who are hurting and in need, and then to take the time to visit with and encourage them. There are many in our churches whose loneliness and abandonment cause them to begin to doubt. They doubt themselves and their own judgment. They doubt the care and concern of others for them. Sometimes they even doubt that God loves them. Even John the Baptist, when confined to prison, alone and out of touch, experienced doubts and had to send a message to Jesus asking if He was really who He claimed to be. There were those who encouraged John the Baptist by delivering the message that Jesus was indeed the Son of God, displaying all of the signs, wonders, and miracles that only God's Son could, delivering the perfect message of hope to a hopeless world. You and I should care about others. We should be known as encouragers. How wonderful it would be if people could give us the nickname of Barnabas the Encourager!

Spiritual Encourager

I suppose the most difficult and, in some ways, the most dangerous way to be an encourager or a Barnabas is by helping those we see

CHAPTER 7

around us in the church who are living in sin and encouraging them in a positive way to repent of those sins and come back to the Lord. Each one of us, at times, has sinned and fallen short of the glory of God. Most of us do so on a regular basis. It cannot help but cause us to wonder when we are blatantly living in a sinful condition and no one from the church comes to visit us or point out our sins and seek to restore us both to fellowship with God and each other. We wonder if anyone really cares about our soul.

Galatians 6:1 tells us that when we see a brother or sister who has fallen and living in sin, that "you who are spiritual should restore him in a spirit of gentleness." It is significant here that the term "spirit of gentleness" is included in our approach to a brother or sister in sin. We can't go to them with guns blazing or a baseball bat in our hand, clubbing them for whatever sin in which they may be involved. We must go to them humbly, with our hat in our hand, and a realization that we, too, are sinners who have failed and fallen. Instead of beating them up, we should encourage them by showing them where their lifestyle may be leading them and letting them know that there are those who care about their souls. We won't be 100 percent successful in trying to restore people to the fellowship of God's church. Not even Jesus or the 12 apostles were successful in restoring Judas. But if we have a genuine, transparent love and concern for those we are approaching who may be living in sin, then we will be far more successful than going to them with a rude, judgmental spirit or attitude.

There are no perfect people, and there are no perfect churches. When I visit people who are considering becoming a member of our congregation, I do not want to paint an unrealistic picture of our church. There is no perfect person or perfect church. I do sincerely believe that our church is striving in every way to serve God, to follow Jesus, and to minister to one another, but the truth is, we all fail and sin from time-to-time.

The Lost

Finally, and most importantly, we need to encourage those who are lost, who do not know our Lord. Jesus came to seek and save the lost. That was His mission. We can do no less than seek and lead to Christ those who are lost. All around us there are friends, relatives, acquaintances, and neighbors who are outside of Christ and lost. Hopefully, most of us try to set a good example to lead them toward Christ, but it takes more than just a good example. We must back up what we say by what we do and by what we ask others to be.

But there is also a responsibility to teach, to bring up the subject of Jesus and His sacrificial death on the cross to save sinners.

I can tell you from experience we will not always be successful in leading those we care about to the Lord. But there will be a satisfaction in knowing that we have taught them and that we have shared with them the love, mercy, and grace of God and how one can become a Christian and the responsibilities of that commitment once it is made. "Go into all the world and preach the gospel" is a commandment directed specifically to us. It isn't just for preachers or elders, it is for those of us who have experienced the salvation found in Jesus.

I am afraid most Christians come to a kind of quiet, inner reconciliation that they either can't or won't try to reach those who are lost around them because of fear, doubt, or embarrassment. We have a gentleman in our church who attended occasionally for many years. But it was only after one of our members went to him and shared with him his love for this gentleman and the gospel that this man, in his late sixties, became a Christian. He now attends every service, is active in many of the programs of the church, and has become a true encourager himself, visiting those who are sick or disabled and sharing his faith with those he knows who are lost. Our prayer should be that we should never become so complacent or indifferent that we cannot see

CHAPTER 7

the needs of others, and that we would want in every way to become a Barnabas, an encourager, and when people speak of us, they speak of us as being helpful and encouraging. The need is certainly there. We live in a world filled with hurting people, looking for someone to encourage them and lift them up. Will you become that person—a Barnabas?

Questions

1. What is the sad attitude of many Christians as they grow older?
2. Do you ever feel lonely or neglected?
3. Do you have good friends, especially Christian friends, who are encouraging to you? If so, how do they encourage you?
4. Discuss those people in Paul's life that he mentions in the various passages in our lesson and how they were a true encouragement to Paul.
5. What was Barnabas's name before it was changed by the apostles?
6. What was Barnabas's first recorded act of encouragement?
7. How was Barnabas instrumental in Paul's being accepted by the Jerusalem church? (Acts 9:27)
8. When Paul and Barnabas had a disagreement concerning John Mark, what was the Christian solution to the problem?
9. What were the positive results of Paul and Barnabas separating and going in two different directions? How does this relate to us today when we have disagreements with our brothers and sisters?
10. What were the indications that Paul later realized the value and importance of John Mark?
11. What is one of our greatest needs in the church today?
12. Name some encouraging people you know and how this makes your life better.

13. What is the most important way we can encourage one another as we grow older?

14. How should we encourage our brothers and sisters who have fallen away and are currently living in sin? What should be our attitude in dealing with them?

15. How can we encourage those who are lost, who have never become a Christian?

16. Do you believe that the encouragement you give to those who are weak and lost will have eternal consequences?

CHAPTER 8

ADJUSTING TO CHANGE

A Little Wisdom

"You cannot always control what happens to you, but you can control your attitude toward what happens to you, and in that you will be mastering change rather than allowing it to master you." (Brian Tracy)

"Not everything we face can be changed, but nothing can be changed until we face it." (James Baldwin, poet)

Real friends are those who, when you've made a fool of yourself, don't feel you've done a permanent job.

"Love bears all things, believes all things, hopes all things, endures all things. Love never ends. As for prophecies, they will pass away; as for tongues, they will cease; as for knowledge, it will pass away" (1 Corinthians 13:7,8).

One who has difficulty adjusting to change, or who is extremely resistant to any change, will usually have problems coping with many of life's situations. Change is constant and dependable. Most everything changes regularly. The only exception is the Godhead. Our mirrors are a constant reminder of change. It seems our appearance is continually changing in subtle ways. That change accelerates when we reach our 40s, 50s, 60s and beyond. One looking in the mirror at 60 can often hardly recognize photographs of himself at 20. Change is inevitable, and the ability to adequately cope with change is essential in the aging process.

CHAPTER 8

The Prodigal Son—Needed Change (Luke 15:11-32)

There are changes that take place during our lives because of the circumstances of our immediate situation. In Luke 15:11-32, the prodigal son had everything he could have possibly wanted or needed, but still he wanted more. So, he began his life of sin and indulgence, going into the far country, away from home and those who loved and cared for him. He became engulfed in passion, pride, and pursuit of pleasure in every form. The end of that road he traveled was a dead end. He woke up having spent all of his money, his so-called friends had deserted him; he was hungry, rejected, and depressed. As he wallowed with the pigs, vying for a little bit of slop, the Bible says "he came to himself," realized that his circumstances were of his own making, and that he had a life waiting for him far better than the one he had chosen. He began the long trek home, no doubt regretting the need to apologize for his waywardness, but also fully understanding its necessity. He was greeted with open arms, forgiveness, and a place back in the family. This was a lesson hard learned, but one that has been an inspiration to millions of people through the years: Sometimes making our own bed is a guarantee of restless nights and little or no sleep. So we come to ourselves, and we realize where our real happiness, security, and purpose lie, and we return to the Lord. All conversion and repentance is based on this kind of change, and it is essential change if we are to find our true place and purpose here and prepare for hereafter.

Life's continuum begins with each of us being completely dependent on someone else. As we move from one stage to another in our lives, we can see these changes, and sometimes even welcome them. We move from preschool to first grade, to junior high, to high school and graduation, and then either more school or accepting a job, often followed by marriage and then family, buying a house and making a home. All these different life stages involve change.

Recently I conducted a worship service at one of our local independent living centers. One of the ladies, whom I had not seen before, came up and said she was moving into the center the following day, but she wanted to get a feel for it beforehand. So she had come for a second tour. She saw us gathered for worship and came in. After our worship, she came up to me and said, "I am more frightened than I ever have been in my life. I am leaving my home of 51 years because of the death of my husband and my inability to keep it up. This is the most difficult change of my life." She sobbed as she talked. I could see the fear she was experiencing. Certainly some changes are far more difficult than others, partly because of our age, and partly because of the significance and reasons for the change. I did what I could to reassure her that I knew many of the residents and that they were very kind and considerate people, many of whom were there for the same reasons she was. I told her that all of her needs would be met, her medications would be provided at the right time, the food in the facility was delicious, and she would have many, many friends she could see as often as she wanted. After 20 or 30 minutes of listening to and reassuring her, she seemed calmer. The last thing she said as I left was, "You know, I don't think it's going to be as bad as I imagined."

Often, we imagine the worst about many of the significant changes in life, especially in older age. There is a sense of loss of control, a feeling of having to accept a choice that was not our first one. Most of the time, after these changes are made and we have experienced a period of adjustment, we find that they have worked out better than we have imagined, and that they are actually comfortable and safe changes for us. Given the choice of doing it over again, we would make the same decision.

Paul—Revelation Change (Acts 9:1-19)

Paul's radical change was the result of revelation, and it was a most beneficial change both for himself and for the millions of

CHAPTER 8

people he had influenced over the years. Acts 9 begins with the statement, "But Saul, still breathing threats and murder against the disciples of the Lord, went to the high priest and asked him for letters to the synagogues at Damascus, so that if he found any belonging to the Way, men or women, he might bring them bound to Jerusalem" (Acts 9:1, 2). Everything Paul did, he did in good conscience, even when he was persecuting Christians. But once he saw the light on the Damascus road and realized the error of his ways, he made a complete, dramatic change, and went from being a Christian persecutor to a proclaimer of Christ. Paul had to give up so much as a result of his radical change, but he gained even more than what he had to sacrifice—his family, close friends, and political and religious connections. Paul considered all of what he gave up as only refuse (Philippians 3:8). Because of what God revealed to him through Jesus on that Damascus road, he became a changed man for the better and spent the rest of his life preaching and teaching the good news of "the Way" he had persecuted.

When we have God's Word revealed to us through the Bible, what we need to do and how we need to live, we should take it as seriously as Paul did. And when our lives do not fit the pattern revealed in the Bible, we need to make whatever changes are necessary to do God's will, recognizing it is what is best for us here and certainly hereafter.

We sometimes realize that we are making a mistake proceeding on our present course of action. So we stop, reverse our action, and go in another direction, avoiding many problems. The entire concept of conversion and repentance involves dramatic change. Our human nature often prompts us to be selfish and live a life devoted simply to pleasure and prosperity. But sooner or later, we usually realize there are more important things in life than self-gratification. Even after becoming a Christian we will encounter a constant series of adjustments in which we realize that we have continued to miss the mark even after our initial decision to change. There are small, subtle changes and repentances all along the way for the Christian. Each of these times of awareness of the need for change hopefully makes us a better person. The transformation from sinner to saint is not instantaneous, because often after becoming a Christian, we revert to our sinful old nature or become aware of practices we need to either do or undo because of our better understanding of God's Word.

When we are young, there is often excitement related to change—a new job, a move to a new city, attending a new school, meeting new people. If there were no change, if we lived in a world of constant sameness, it would be a dull existence. Our attitude toward change, to a large extent, determines the success or failure of those changes. Voluntary changes are more easily accepted than forced ones. Sometimes because of health problems, the death of loved ones, financial reverses, divorces, or job losses, we are forced to make decisions and changes to which we may take a little longer to adjust. But even in these instances, as we look back on them several years later, we see that they were decisions that helped us to grow to be a better person and end up in a better place.

Significant change starts with a new life, not just a new leaf. The best change any of us can make starts with a new birth, becoming a new person, walking in a different direction, and dumping all of the sin and guilt we'd acquired up until the time of our baptism and the washing away and cleansing of our sins (Romans 6). We do away with the old and happily embrace the new. Second Corinthians 5:17 gloriously proclaims, "Therefore, if anyone is in Christ, he is a new creation. The old has passed away; behold, the new has come." Our saving faith centers around turning over an old life for a new one. John 3:3 says we are born again, and genuine change is not a destination, but rather a process. Philippians 1:6 reminds us, "I am sure of this, that he who began a good work in you will bring it to completion at the day

CHAPTER 8

of Jesus Christ." "And we all, with unveiled face, beholding the glory of the Lord, are being transformed into the same image from one degree of glory to another. For this comes from the Lord who is the Spirit" (2 Corinthians 3:18).

Every time we let go of one thing, we should be grasping another.

> "But that is not the way you learned about Christ!—assuming that you have heard about him and were taught in him, as the truth is in Jesus, to put off your old self, which belongs to your former manner of life and is corrupt through deceitful desires, and to be renewed in the spirit of your minds, and to put on the new self, created after the likeness of God in true righteousness and holiness" (Ephesians 4:20-24).

Thomas Rainer, a Christian author, listed reasons why we are afraid of change. (1) Because we are stubborn. (2) Because we are trapped. (3) Because we are comfortable. (4) Because we are afraid. (5) Because change sometimes hurts. (6) Because it takes away our power.

> "…having the eyes of your hearts enlightened, that you may know what is the hope to which he has called you, what are the riches of his glorious inheritance in the saints, and what is the immeasurable greatness of his power toward us who believe, according to the working of his great might that he worked in Christ when he raised him from the dead and seated him at his right hand in the heavenly places" (Ephesians 1:18-20).

> "But if there is no resurrection of the dead, then not even Christ has been raised. And if Christ has not been raised, then our preaching is in vain and your faith is in vain" (1 Corinthians 15:13,14).

Joseph—Forced Change (Genesis 37:12-36)
Joseph, who at an early age had managed to offend his brothers to the extent they were ready to kill him, found himself in a position in which his world changed instantaneously. Instead of killing

him, as most of the brothers wanted to, Judah recommended they sell him to a group of traders who happened by their way. This is a radical change—to go from security, comfort, and what he believed to be a loving family to being betrayed, almost killed, and sold into slavery. Through the selfishness and sinfulness of his brothers, Joseph found himself alone and in a strange country. Somehow he had the resilience (I believe, no doubt, because of his early training and teaching and the love his father had shown him) to be resilient enough to maintain a balanced and optimistic attitude, even under the most despairing circumstances. At every turn, he would take a seemingly disastrous circumstance and turn it into a blessing. We know that one of the major reasons he was able to accomplish this was because of his faith in God and God's faithfulness to him. It would have been so easy for him, once betrayed, to have begun a life of continual bad decisions and mistakes. Instead, Joseph embraced the change and was able to achieve the highest success. It is amazing what God can do with people who, though they have been neglected and abused and cast aside for one reason or the other, have made the best of their unwanted life changes. There are some changes over which we have little or no control. Under those circumstances, we have to maintain a strong faith in God, an understanding of right and wrong, and a decision to do what we can to better our lives and the lives of those around us, even under harsh circumstances.

Change is often essential to experiencing the best that this life and the life to come can offer. There is some wonderful news for every Christian. We can change our lives for the better simply by changing the way we think, re-educating our thought processes. This re-education comes through an understanding study of God's Word. When we are changed by God, we are changed by God's Word. It is His Word that defines for us the kind of person we need to be. When our thoughts become His thoughts, it creates positive changes in us. "As [a man] thinks in

CHAPTER 8

his heart, so is he" (Proverbs 23:7, NKJV). We literally become like what we think about. Unfortunately for most of the world, their thought changes come about because of what they see on TV, hear on the radio, search for on the web, see in the movies, or read in newspapers or magazines. To be sure, there is good and bad in all of these areas of communication. But the life-changing experiences we need most are to be found in a study of God's Word. The commandments, examples, principles, and inferences all guide us to a better life.

Broad Is the Way
It saddens me as I look back to all of the Christians I have known and realize that so many of them have made changes in the wrong direction. After having embraced saving changes that Christ brings about in our lives, the pressures and cares of the world caused them to change again to a life away from God. Growing up, we had a strong church family and an excellent Bible class program. There were 16 junior high students in my Bible class who had become Christians. All but three of those have left their first love. In college, there were more than 20 of my close friends who planned to be ministers. Most of them went on to serve in the church for a period of time. Some of them left the ministry because of moral improprieties, others because of faith issues, and still others left to pursue occupations outside the ministry, as I did in becoming a therapist. But the point is, of those who originally intended to be ministers, only three remained ministers until retirement. The pressures of our world are strong and, like a magnet, they pull us away to distracted ways of life. Certainly we can serve God effectively and faithfully in occupations unrelated to ministry, but our world today needs faithful, effective ministers to fill our pulpits and challenge and inspire us.

No one is born a faithful Christian. We are all born sinners. Romans 3 teaches us . . .

> "...as it is written: 'None is righteous, no, not one; no one understands; no one seeks for God. All have turned aside; together they have become worthless; no one does good, not even one.' 'Their throat is an open grave; they use their tongues to deceive.' 'The venom of asps is under their lips.' 'Their mouth is full of curses and bitterness.' 'Their feet are swift to shed blood; in their paths are ruin and misery, and the way of peace they have not known.' 'There is no fear of God before their eyes.' Now we know that whatever the law says it speaks to those who are under the law, so that every mouth may be stopped, and the whole world may be held accountable to God. For by works of the law no human being will be justified in his sight, since through the law comes knowledge of sin. But now the righteousness of God has been manifested apart from the law, although the Law and the Prophets bear witness to it—the righteousness of God through faith in Jesus Christ for all who believe. For there is no distinction: for all have sinned and fall short of the glory of God" (10-23).

Every one of us needs to change and be born again so that we may receive eternal life.

> "Now there was a man of the Pharisees named Nicodemus, a ruler of the Jews. This man came to Jesus by night and said to him, 'Rabbi, we know that you are a teacher come from God, for no one can do these signs that you do unless God is with him.' Jesus answered him, 'Truly, truly, I say to you, unless one is born again he cannot see the kingdom of God.' Nicodemus said to him, 'How can a man be born when he is old? Can he enter a second time into his mother's womb and be born?' Jesus answered, 'Truly, truly, I say to you, unless one is born of water and the Spirit, he cannot enter the kingdom of God.'"
> "For God so loved the world, that he gave his only Son, that whoever believes in him should not perish but have eternal life" (John 3:1-5,16).

As Christians, we often need to begin again and change. David prayed for the opportunity of a new beginning in Psalm 51. The prodigal son came to himself and realized he needed to make a change by leaving the pigpen and returning home. Apart from

CHAPTER 8

these spiritual changes, each of us, as we grow older, will experience the reality of change—changes in our appearance, our health, our living arrangements, our friends, our attitudes, and other subtle changes that require us to adapt or be overcome.

God, Jesus, and the Spirit Never Change
"Jesus Christ is the same yesterday and today and forever" (Hebrews 13:8). It is comforting that in a world filled with constant change, some good, some bad, that there is perfection that never changes. God never changes. His promises are true and faithful, and our final change—that is, the change from a corruptible body to an incorruptible body—will allow us to spend forever with God and our brothers and sisters in Christ in a place of perpetual happiness, joy, and gladness, where all of these difficult changes we experienced on earth will have ended. There will be no more sickness or sadness or sorrow, only perpetual pleasantness and happiness.

> "Then I saw a new heaven and a new earth, for the first heaven and the first earth had passed away, and the sea was no more. And I saw the holy city, new Jerusalem, coming down out of heaven from God, prepared as a bride adorned for her husband. And I heard a loud voice from the throne saying, 'Behold, the dwelling place of God is with man. He will dwell with them, and they will be his people, and God himself will be with them as their God. He will wipe away every tear from their eyes, and death shall be no more, neither shall there be mourning, nor crying, nor pain anymore, for the former things have passed away'" (Revelation 21:1-4).

Remember always to pray for the wisdom and strength to accept the positive changes that God places before us.

Conclusion
Life is always changing. It never stays the same. It doesn't matter whether we are young, middle-aged, or older—change is always a reality. In fact, it is inevitable. It is possible, though, to make

needed changes without becoming overwhelmed and stressed out. These principles will apply to positive changes in our lives as well as some unwanted changes that are forced upon us. Some call them coping skills, others refer to the ability to "roll with the punches," and still others may define them as flexibility.

The first one is to fully accept the changes that are necessary and inevitable. Like so many transitions in life, the harder you fight against them, the more difficult they become. Sometimes we have to just let go and embrace the inevitable. You've probably heard the expression, "Let go and let God." Don't judge yourself by others, because each of us experiences change in different ways. One person may handle it one way, which is acceptable, and another person may handle it in a different way, which is also acceptable. You should also depend on those people around you whom you trust. Go to them for advice and counsel. You may not agree with or accept everything they say, but at the very least, you will get their support in whatever decision you may make. The support of good friends is essential in making difficult changes in our lives. Often this friendship group dynamic can offer sound advice and positive support and reinforcement.

Second, even in the middle of significant change, we need to try to maintain as familiar a routine as possible. We certainly do not want to try to change too much at one time. We do not want to feel overwhelmed thinking that everything in our life has changed. Maintain a regular routine and rely on those changes you have already made earlier in life that have proven helpful and successful. Try to remember these previous changes that worked out well and how you went about making them, what methods you used, how you felt during the process, and what brought peace to you concerning these changes. These principles are all a part of learning and remembering coping skills that have helped us throughout our lives. Don't allow people to tell you how to feel about these changes. Feel what you feel. Express your feelings.

CHAPTER 8

Do not suppress them. It takes time to mentally, emotionally, physically, and spiritually adjust to life changes. You don't want to get stuck in indecision or procrastination, nor do you want to feel sorry for yourself about having to make difficult changes. Work through the emotional trauma of change in a reasonable way and length of time. And don't forget to pray! "Pray without ceasing" (1 Thessalonians 5:17).

Food For Thought

"Let us then with confidence draw near to the throne of grace, that we may receive mercy and find grace to help in time of need" (Hebrews 4:16).

"These things I command you, so that you will love one another" (John 15:17).

"Therefore I tell you, whatever you ask in prayer, believe that you have received it and it will be yours" (Mark 11:24).

"Until now you have asked nothing in may name. Ask, and you will receive, that your joy may be full" (John 16:24).

"The Lord is near to all who call on him, to all who call on him in truth" (Psalm 145:18).

"...casting all your anxieties on him, because he cares for you" (1 Peter 5:7).

"...do not be anxious about anything, but in everything by prayer and supplication with thanksgiving let your requests be made known to God. And the peace of God, which surpasses all understanding, will guard your hearts and your minds in Christ Jesus" (Philippians 4:6, 7).

Questions

1. Do older people often have difficulty adjusting to change? If so, why?
2. At any age, is change avoidable? Discuss, and give a biblical example of needed change.
3. Why is changing where we live so uncomfortable, and why is it sometimes necessary?
4. Why do we often imagine the worst about changes in life, especially as we grow older?
5. Give an example of change that takes place when we are confronted with God's Word (Acts 9:1-19).
6. Even when we realize we are headed in the wrong direction, and we know change is necessary, why is it often difficult to make those changes?
7. How is our attitude toward change different when we are younger than it is when we are older?
8. What are the six reasons Thomas Ranier says we resist change?
9. What is a biblical example of forced change (changes made against our will)?
10. How can we adequately survive such changes?
11. What are some changes we make that have eternal negative consequences in our lives (hint: *Leaving Our First Love*)?
12. What never changes? How does that give us security and comfort?

CHAPTER 9

LIVE AS POSITIVELY AS POSSIBLE

A Little Humor

Oh, yeah, I've got O.C.D. I'm old, cranky, and dangerous, so don't mess with me!

The Good and Bad of Life

Is attitude a biblical subject? Does attitude matter? Life is made up of both positive and negative thoughts, people, and events. Yet life can be made better or worse by our attitude—how we think. There are times in our lives when it is appropriate, even right, to be negative. For example, we should always decline things that are wrong, harmful, or sinful.

Old age tests our faith and attitude. Often we do not have the strength or stamina of youth. We may be tested by illness, relationship problems, financial problems, or a host of other issues that seem to overwhelm us. More than ever before in our lives we must trust God and His care and do everything we possibly can to maintain a positive, healthy attitude.

Some time ago my wife and I were going to a doctor's appointment. As we got off the elevator at the medical building, there was an elderly gentleman who held the door open for five or six people. One lady, who was supporting an older lady, said "Thank you. It's nice to know there are still gentlemen." To which the older lady she was assisting said, "There are no gentlemen." The younger lady replied, "Yes, there are." And the older lady said, "I'm paying you to help me get around, not to tell me how to think."

CHAPTER 9

As we stepped off the elevator, I think everyone was struck with the same thought: Some people, no matter the circumstances or situation, will always look for the negative.

Solomon

Solomon had every reason in the world to be happy and positive. Instead, he chose to be negative and depressive. No one had acquired as much wealth or as many possessions as he, but none of these brought him happiness. His possessions possessed him. His thinking patterns were almost exclusively negative. He could take a positive situation or a beautiful building or garden and find only the negative in it, stating, "It's all vanity, just vanity."

Paul

Paul was, on the other hand, largely a positive person.

> "Rejoice in the Lord always; again I will say, rejoice. Let your reasonableness be known to everyone. The Lord is at hand; do not be anxious about anything, but in everything by prayer and supplication with thanksgiving let your requests be made known to God. And the peace of God, which surpasses all understanding, will guard your hearts and your minds in Christ Jesus. Finally, brothers, whatever is true, whatever is honorable, whatever is just, whatever is pure, whatever is lovely, whatever is commendable, if there is any excellence, if there is anything worthy of praise, think about these things. What you have learned and received and heard and seen in me—practice these things, and the God of peace will be with you" (Philippians 4:4-9).

Paul was able to adjust well to the circumstances of life, both good and bad, and maintain a positive perspective.

> "Not that I am speaking of being in need, for I have learned in whatever situation I am to be content. I know how to be brought low, and I know how to abound. In any and every circumstance, I have learned the secret of facing plenty and hunger, abundance and need. I can do all things through him who strengthens me" (Philippians 4:11-13).

If we truly believe that we can do all things through Him who strengthens us (Jesus), then that in and of itself will make us a more positive person.

Paul was a busy person, always active in a godly pursuit. Even in his early life, when his name was Saul, he vigorously pursued what he believed to be the truth, albeit in an extremely aggressive manner. Busy people tend to be more positive. It is important even as we age that we maintain a feeling of usefulness by staying busy. We can be busy visiting our friends and neighbors, reading good books, or forgiving others who may have wronged us and, as a result, overcoming bitterness and anger. We can spend time in Bible study and, because of retirement, more time in prayer. We can volunteer at church or other charitable organizations. There are so many positive things we can do to enrich our lives and the lives of others.

Every time you speak, try to speak with a positive, uplifting comment. If you do say something to your spouse or a friend in anger or just negativity, ask that person to forgive you, and assure her you will try to be more pleasant. Consider stopping complaining and starting to compliment. You might help your children, telling them every day how much you love them, even if they live far away. Tell your friends how much you appreciate them and all they have done for you throughout your life. Consider doing something positive at church. You might teach a Bible class or be a classroom helper. Write notes to the ministers and elders, telling them how much you appreciate the time, effort, and energy they put into God's church. You could write to those who are absent from worship.

Often as we grow older, we can become satisfied with being a part-time (or less) Christian. But growing older is an opportunity to transition from one kind of work to another. In everything we do, we should try to be encouraging and uplifting. Maintaining a positive attitude is probably more helpful to us than to anyone else who may happen to observe the positivity we exhibit.

CHAPTER 9

Living in a Negative World

We live in an extremely negative world. War, crime, terrorism, alcoholism, abortion, divorce, and illness are just a few of the negative influences that constantly surround us. I personally have had to greatly limit my exposure to the news. Hearing all of the bad in the world once a day is more than enough for me. Yet I know some people who are tuned in to news broadcasts all day, and that negativity can't help but influence one's thinking. Being constantly bombarded with negative messages is one of the disadvantages of living in an age of instant worldwide communication. We become immediately aware of any problem area in the world. Violent acts are reported to us. They enter our homes, workplaces, and cars instantaneously. They are accompanied by graphic video and gory details. It can be overwhelming. As a therapist I can tell you there are many psychological dangers to constant negative input. We literally become what we think about, and we think about those things to which we are constantly exposed. Not only does repeated negativity affect us psychologically, but it can also cause physical problems, and it most certainly affects our attitude, disposition, and spiritual life. The world's negativity promotes anxiety, fear, worry, stress, and often a feeling of helplessness in our not being able to do anything about these situations.

Negative Thinking

Some people will always oppose any good work. Nehemiah discovered this when trying to rebuild the wall around Jerusalem. Nehemiah 4:1, 2 tells us: "Now when Sanballat heard that we were building the wall, he was angry and greatly enraged, and he jeered at the Jews. And he said in the presence of his brothers and of the army of Samaria, 'What are these feeble Jews doing? Will they restore it for themselves? Will they sacrifice? Will they finish up in a day? Will they revive the stones out of the heaps of rubbish, and burned ones at that?'"

Despite opposition, we must remain positive.

"If God is for us, who can be against us?" (Romans 8:31).

"Let not steadfast love and faithfulness forsake you; bind them around your neck; write them on the tablet of your heart. So you will find favor and good success in the sight of God and man. Trust in the Lord with all your heart, and do not lean on your own understanding. In all your ways acknowledge him, and he will make straight your paths" (Proverbs 3:3-6).

"God is our refuge and strength, a very present help in trouble. Therefore we will not fear though the earth gives way, though the mountains be moved into the heart of the sea, though its waters roar and foam, though the mountains tremble at its swelling" (Psalm 46:1-3).

" ...so as to walk in a manner worthy of the Lord, fully pleasing to him: bearing fruit in every good work and increasing in the knowledge of God; being strengthened with all power, according to his glorious might, for all endurance and patience with joy; giving thanks to the Father, who has qualified you to share in the inheritance of the saints in light. He has delivered us from the domain of darkness and transferred us to the kingdom of his beloved Son, in whom we have redemption, the forgiveness of sins" (Colossians 1:10-14).

Paul was in prison at a time when he and Silas were singing and praying to God at midnight, and God powerfully demonstrated His approval of their prayerful, positive attitude. Near the end of his life, Paul was in a Roman prison, with every possible reason to be discouraged, an older man, facing a cold, damp cell. No one would have blamed him if he had feelings of bitterness or remorse. But he didn't. Instead, he had an optimistic outlook and was writing a positive message to the brothers and sisters in Philippi.

"Rejoice in the Lord always; again I will say, rejoice. Let your reasonableness be known to everyone. The Lord is at hand; do not be anxious about anything" (Philippians 4:4,5).

CHAPTER 9

A Parting Thought

My prayer is that each of the books I write will be encouraging and informative to all readers. I know for those of you who are suffering with cancer, heart disease, depression, anxiety, dementia, or any major disease or disorder, it is difficult to remain positive. We sometimes go through periods in our life in which we are overwhelmed by the reality and circumstance of our situation. Certainly one should not feel guilty for an occasional lapse in positive attitude. When one is in the midst of struggling for life or sanity, everything else takes second place. But as I have counseled with people who are terminally ill or suffering emotionally, I have found that the more positive attitude they can maintain, the better off they are at coping with whatever condition they are experiencing. Faith and a positive attitude are closely connected. Some believe they are inseparable. For the Christian, the good news is our eternal destiny is assured and we can change our attitude toward life's adverse circumstances by simply changing our attitude to a more hopeful and faith-based positive outlook. Prayer is essential. We must spend much time in prayer asking for God's guidance, direction, forgiveness, and strength.

Good Advice from Positive People

You don't want to end up being a negative, pessimistic, older person. God's Word, common sense, and the testimony of successful people show the wisdom of a positive, optimistic attitude.

> *"Perpetual optimism is a force multiplier."* (Colin Powell)
>
> *"Attitude is a little thing that makes a big difference."* (Winston Churchill)
>
> *"Keep your face to the sunshine and you cannot see a shadow."* (Helen Keller, who was both blind and deaf)
>
> *"Once you replace negative thoughts with positive ones, you'll start having positive results."* (unknown)

> "Yesterday is not ours to recover, but tomorrow is ours to win or lose." (Lyndon B. Johnson)
>
> "I always like to look on the optimistic side of life, but I am realistic enough to know that life is a very complex matter." (Walt Disney)
>
> "Positive thinking will let you do everything better than negative thinking." (Zig Ziglar)
>
> "Pessimism leads to weakness; optimism to power." (William James)
>
> "You can't make positive choices for the rest of your life without an environment that makes those choices easy, natural, and enjoyable." (Deepak Chopra)
>
> "The thing that lies at the foundation of positive change, the way I see it, is service to a fellow human being." (Lee Iacocca)
>
> "Positive thinking is more than just a tagline. It changes the way we behave, and I firmly believe that when I am positive it not only makes me better but is also makes those around me better." (Harvey Mackay)
>
> "A pessimist sees the difficult in every opportunity, and an optimist sees the opportunity in every difficulty." (Winston Churchill)

Keep Your Eye on Jesus

> "And Peter answered him, 'Lord, if it is you, command me to come to you on the water.' He said, 'Come.' So Peter got out of the boat and walked on the water and came to Jesus. But when he saw the wind, he was afraid, and beginning to sink he cried out, 'Lord, save me.'" (Matthew 14:28-30).

As soon as Peter took his eyes off Jesus and looked at the stormy sea, he began to sink. He could have walked on water as Jesus did, but he lost his focus. Some researchers feel as much as 77 percent of everything we think is negative and, as a result, counterproductive. It truly is easier to be negative than to be positive.

CHAPTER 9

Questions

1. Is attitude a biblical subject? Why does it matter?
2. What is the best way to deal with the negative things we experience?
3. Name ways our positive attitude is tested as we grow older.
4. Discuss biblical examples of both positive and negative attitudes and how they affected the individual.
5. How does our attitude, either positive or negative, affect our spouse and friends?
6. What are some positive things we can do to help at church?
7. How does the negative world in which we live affect our personal attitude?
8. Is limiting our exposure to negative input necessary to maintain a more positive attitude?
9. How does a negative attitude affect us psychologically, physically, and spiritually?
10. Discuss Paul's ability to remain positive and write positive letters to Christians, even while he was imprisoned or in life-threatening situations.
11. Why should we not feel guilty when overwhelmed with a life-threatening disease or situation when we may, for a short time, become negative and depressed?
12. Each of us, when faced with one of life's catastrophes, may experience setbacks in our desire to live a positive life. Discuss how prayer is essential in maintaining our spiritual balance and a positive attitude in life.

CHAPTER 10

THE PRIVILEGE OF BEING A GRANDPARENT

A Little Wisdom

Conscience is God's built-in warning system. Be very happy when it hurts you. Be very worried when it doesn't.

Most people wish to serve God—but only in an advisory capacity.

When God measures a man, He puts the tape around the heart instead of the head.

A marriage may be made in heaven, but the maintenance must be done on earth.

Certain opportunities and privileges come to us at different stages of life. Hopefully, we are well-prepared for these opportunities and special times. One of those special moments is if we become a grandparent. Being a grandparent is both an awesome responsibility and wonderful privilege. Most of the time, it's having fun without major, long-term responsibility. I do admire those grandparents who, when necessity arises, are willing to step up and take over the responsibilities of being a parent. That is a sacrifice that will be well-rewarded in the end.

Grandparents are special. They are supposed to be grand! As we get older and sift through the memories of our past, any memories we may have of our own grandparents are among the most cherished. Sometimes we have heirlooms passed on to us from grandparents and great-grandparents. I have an oak chest of drawers that was in my grandmother Glover's guest room, and when I would go there as a child, I would pilfer through the drawers where my uncle had stored many of his favorite collectibles when he went to war. Unfortunately, he and another of my uncles never returned home. He left behind a Zane Grey collection and several pocketknives, baseballs, etc. When my grandmother and grandfather passed away, and I was allowed to have the old oak chest, it became my favorite piece of furniture, bringing back many memories of childhood visits to my grandparents. You may have many memories of your own grandparents and special times spent with them. Grandparents are often a big part of who we are today. Godly grandparents are a great asset to any family. Usually grandparents are celebrated on Grandparents' Day, the first Sunday in September after Labor Day. We honor mothers and fathers, and we also honor our grandparents with a day of remembrance. But we need to remember good mothers, fathers, and grandparents every day as they are among the best role models for children.

Grandparents of the Bible

In Genesis 48 and 49, we read the account of Jacob's blessing his sons and grandsons. During this lengthy blessing, he reminded his sons of his concerns and hopes for their future. He was trying to instill in them a strong sense of responsibility. His advice was direct and forceful. But when he blessed his grandsons, Ephraim and Manasseh, the blessings were free from criticism and regret. He began the blessing by saying, "The God before whom my fathers Abraham and Isaac walked, the God who has been my shepherd all my life long to this day, the angel who has redeemed me from all evil..." (Genesis 48:15,16). He then gave them a three-part blessing. "Bless the boys; and in them let my name be carried on, and the name of my fathers Abraham and Isaac; and let them grow into a multitude in the midst of the earth" (Genesis 48:16). Jacob wanted them to have a great future and to keep God's teachings and blessings alive. I wish we had more traditions where we pronounced blessings upon our children and grandchildren, especially as we approach the end of our life.

In our congregation we have a special blessing of newborn children every quarter. All the children born during that time are brought up with their parents and siblings before the congregation and hear this passage read:

> "Hear, O Israel: the Lord our God, the Lord is one. You shall love the Lord your God with all your heart and with all your soul and with all your might. And these words that I command you today shall be on your heart. You shall teach them diligently to your children, and shall talk of them when you sit in your house, and when you walk by the way, and when you lie down, and when you rise. You shall bind them as a sign on your hand, and they shall be as frontlets between your eyes. You shall write them on the doorposts of your house and on your gates" (Deuteronomy 4:6-9).

After the Scripture reading, all of the parents are asked if they will do their best to rear their children in the nurture and admonition of the Lord, dedicating the children and themselves to God and His Word. It is a special time, and one I think that encourages the parents to be the best examples they possibly can and reminds them of what an awesome responsibility they have in rearing their children. Grandparents would do well to renew the dedication of their children, including their grandchildren. Possibly we can do that more informally, by just sharing with our grandchildren what our hopes, dreams, and aspirations are for them and reminding our children and grandchildren of our heritage—where they have come from and who they are. I can remember my mother saying on several occasions, when I was getting ready to go out as a teenager, "Remember who you are!" That was sound advice because, as Christians, we need to not only remember who we are but pass on that blessing to our children and grandchildren.

Our heritage and roots are important elements in the education of our children and grandchildren. After my parents and

CHAPTER 10

grandparents had all passed, I regretted not having asked more questions about our family history. Little things in which we have only a passing interest, if at all, when we are younger become important questions to be answered as we get older. So while we have time and opportunity, let's share with our children and grandchildren what is most important to us and something of the history of our past.

Enoch

In Genesis 5 we read an account of Enoch, the son of Jared, and the father of Methuselah. Methuselah was the father of Lamech, and Lamech was the father of Noah. Enoch was a faithful man of God. Because he passed that faith on, five generations later Noah became a great man of God who saved the future of mankind. Noah and the faithfulness of his family were all that stood between extinction and mankind.

Margaret Mead, a well-respected anthropologist, has said, "Somehow we have to get older people, grandparents, widows, widowers, spinsters, bachelors, back close to children if we are to restore a sense of community and a knowledge of the past and a sense of the future to today's children." This is one of the privileges of being a grandparent.

Proverbs 17:6 tells us, "Grandchildren are the crown of the aged...." We need to be a good example to our grandchildren. Let them hear you pray. Let them see you reading the Bible. Let them observe you being a good, kind, compassionate person.

Timothy

Godly grandparents pass on their faith. Anyone can be a grandparent, but not everyone is a good, godly grandparent. Paul reminded Timothy how he came to faith. "I am reminded of your sincere faith, a faith that dwelt first in your grandmother Lois and your mother Eunice and now, I am sure, dwells in you as well" (2 Timothy 1:5). This passage describes the faith in God that has been passed through three generations. Paul uses the word *sincere*, meaning this faith is genuine, well-lived. Grandmother Lois was what she claimed to be. She was a faithful follower of God. You have to possess something to pass it on. Lois possessed a sincere faith. Because it was real and a deep part of her life, she was able to pass it on. Children have a kind of sixth sense and are able to spot insincerity. They seem to intuitively know whether you believe what you say and are living what you claim. The best gifts you can give your grandchildren aren't toys or gadgets, but a deep and abiding faith in God.

In 2 Timothy 3:14, 15, Paul makes his point clear. "But as for you, continue in what you have learned and have firmly believed, knowing from whom you learned it [your grandmother Lois, your mother Eunice, and myself] and how from childhood you have been acquainted with the sacred writings, which are able to make you wise for salvation through faith in Christ Jesus." That is the greatest gift of all—the gift of faith.

Ruth

The book of Ruth is a wonderful love story, but it is more than that. It is a continuation of the genealogy of Christ. Ruth and Boaz were married, and Ruth gave birth to Obed.

> "So Boaz took Ruth, and she became his wife. And he went in to her, and the Lord gave her conception, and she bore a son. Then the women said to Naomi, 'Blessed be the Lord, who has not left you this day without a redeemer, and may his name be renowned in Israel! He shall be to you a restorer of life and a nourisher of your old age, for your daughter-in-law who loves you, who is more to you than seven sons, has given birth to him.' Then Naomi took the child and laid him on her lap and became his nurse. And the women of the neighborhood gave him a name, saying, 'A son has been born to Naomi.' They named him Obed. He was the father of Jesse, the father of David" (Ruth 4:13-17).

At this point, Grandmother Naomi seems to have taken center stage as the curtain closes on the book of Ruth. Obed was the

CHAPTER 10

grandfather of David. The genealogy of David is given in Ruth 4:18-22. There is no doubt that Naomi, the grandmother who showed great faith in God, was one of the great stars of the book of Ruth, and she is last pictured with her grandson in her lap, surrounded by encouraging friends, and aware that Obed is a part of the bloodline of David and Jesus.

Truly "grandchildren are the crown of the aged" (Proverbs 17:6). Someone has said, "Your children may have kept you poor, but their children will make you rich." We may never know the eternal consequences of the influence we have on our children and grandchildren. A 9-year-old girl wrote this description of grandmothers:

"A grandmother is a lady who has no children of her own... so she likes other people's little girls. A grandfather is a man grandmother. He goes for walks with boys and talks about fishing, tractors, and stuff like that. Grandmas don't have to do anything except be there. They're old, so they shouldn't play hard, or run. It is enough if they drive us to the market, where the pretend horse is, and have lots of quarters ready. Or, if they take us for walks, they slow down at things like pretty leaves or caterpillars. They never, ever say 'Hurry up.' Usually they are fat, but not too fat to tie the kids' shoes. They wear glasses and funny underwear. They can take their teeth out. They don't have to be smart, only answer questions like, 'Why do dogs hate cats?' and 'How come God isn't married?' They don't talk baby talk like some people do, because it is hard to understand. When they read to us, they don't skip pages. Everybody should try to have one, especially if you don't have television, because grandmas are the only grown ups who have got time."

It is a blessed privilege to be a good grandparent.

If grandparents are gone, aunts, uncles, and even cousins can become surrogate grandparents.

The word *grand* in grandparents is quite appropriate. "Grand" children make "grand" parents, and vice versa.

There are approximately 50 million grandparents in the U.S. Many of these men and women play increasingly positive roles in their grandchildren's lives. Grandparents can serve in many different capacities in the life of a grandchild—mentor, role model, teacher, spiritual advisor, comforter—all of these roles from grandparents are important, but different than the same roles from parents.

Arthur Kornhaber, author of *The Grandparent Guide*, says, "The grandparent-grandchild bond is second in emotional importance only to the bond between parents and children." He continues, "It is the only relationship in which people are crazy about each other simply because they're breathing. Grandparents and grandchildren are hardwired to connect in ways different from parents and children. They have this adoration and unconditional love and joy in one another's existence."

Gillian Kruse, a freelance writer from Houston, Texas, lists 10 things that grandparents can do to help their grandchildren:

1. Grandparents can give a sense of history to their grandchildren. They can fill in details and facts of the early lives of the parents and other relatives. Children can learn what it was like when their parents were growing up.
2. They can learn new skill sets. Grandparents often have skills such as sewing, gardening, baking, farming, woodworking, etc. These are passed on to grandchildren. Not only will these skills give added confidence, but it will teach them to use the talents they have. Our grandchildren and great-grandchildren call Donna, my wife, many times during the week for advice on illnesses in the family, for recipes, or for advice on how to handle a particular situation with one of the grandchildren, which brings us to our third quality of grandparenting.
3. Grandparents can impart wisdom. They have learned many life lessons, often hard lessons, and they can give good

advice for children and grandchildren to avoid mistakes and also profit from the successes of grandparents. Grandparents have a way of soothing grandchildren and making them feel everything is going to be okay.

4. Grandparents can also give a specific, detailed account, not only of history in general, but family history in particular. Finding our roots is important. Knowing where we come from, our ancestors' nationality, their names, occupations, and aspirations, are all important pieces of information to the puzzle of who we are. Especially important is passing on humorous stories or stories involving famous relatives.

5. Humor. Parents have to take life, and their children's behavior, seriously. But grandparents can be a little lighter in their dealing with grandchildren, and through humor, they can pass on an important ingredient in the grandchild's personality.

6. Listening. Grandparents may have more time to listen than parents, and listening is important in a child's life. Grandparents' willingness to listen to their grandchildren creates an important bond in their life.

7. Grandparents can play games with their grandchildren. Pitching a ball, playing card games, and taking part in board games—all of these harken back to earlier days of the grandparents rather than the highly technical gadget games of today.

8. Grandparents can offer emotional support. They can be a sounding board for their grandchildren's frustrations and can offer good advice on how important it is to listen to parents and understand why they make the decisions they do.

9. Grandparents can teach their grandchildren not to sweat the small stuff. Most grandparents have lived long enough to realize they do not need to get upset over little things. Life is too short, and most of the time, the things that frustrate us the most have a way of working themselves out. But in

the life of a grandchild, some small issues become life and death issues. By both example and teaching, grandparents can point out that a positive attitude toward life events brings everything into better perspective.

10. Do not allow the art of letter-writing to fade away. In this day of texting, tweeting, and such, it is important that grandchildren learn to take time and thought to putting their ideas and concerns on paper. Letters and postcards to grandchildren can become treasured souvenirs and the source of great encouragement at the grandparents' passing.

Grandparenting comes with many years of experience and wisdom that needs to be shared with grandchildren. We simply need to take the time to really get to know our grandchildren and share in their guidance for healthy, mature adults.

Questions

1. What is one of the most important privileges and opportunities that comes to us as we grow older?
2. How are grandparents special? What are some specific things we can do to affect the future of our grandchildren?
3. Discuss Jacob's blessing his sons and grandsons as described in Genesis 48 and 49.
4. How do you feel about having a blessing for newborn children in the congregation, using Deuteronomy 4:6-9 as a dedication and challenge for the parents as well as grandparents?
5. Discuss teaching our grandchildren the important elements of our education, early home life, and spiritual heritage.
6. Discuss how Enoch was a true blessing to his future generations.
7. Discuss Timothy and the great influence of his mother and grandmother (2 Timothy 3:14, 15).
8. Discuss how Ruth was influenced by a wonderful mother-in-law and the grandmother of hers and Boaz's child.

CHAPTER 10

9. What is the significance of Naomi's grandson in the genealogy of Jesus?
10. What are 10 ways grandparents can have a positive effect on their grandchildren?
11. Discuss how being a grandparent has enriched your personal life.

CHAPTER 11

THE IMPORTANCE OF LOVE

As I look back over the past 50 plus years of preaching, teaching, and writing, I am amazed at how many times I have written and spoken on the topic of love. Yet, in another way, I shouldn't be surprised at all, since love is the core foundation and motivation for everything we do in service to God and one another. Faith, hope, and love are the secure foundations of our Christian Commitment, yet love is the greatest of all (1 Corinthians 13:13). It is that one eternal quality that will be transferred with us to our heavenly home.

Defining the word *love* has always been a challenge because there are so many different perspectives and definitions of the word. There is only one definition given by inspiration that encompasses all of the complexities of the word.

> "Love is patient and kind; love does not envy or boast; it is not arrogant or rude. It does not insist on its own way; it is not irritable or resentful; it does not rejoice at wrongdoing, but rejoices with the truth. Love bears all things, believes all things, hopes all things, endures all things. Love never ends" (1 Corinthians 13:4-8a).

The motivation for everything we do as God's people destined for heaven must be love. Any good we do for any motivation other than love has little or no eternal value. The Bible is full of encouragements, examples, and commandments to love. Ecclesiastes 3:8 states there is "a time to love." Any time is a time to love.

This is a subject that affects every one of us all of our lives, regardless of our age. Love must be the motivation for our

CHAPTER 11

Christian walk. No one is exempt from the essential need to be motivated by love. The world is full of people who are motivated by self-centered hatred or selfishness.

Love is powerful. It can change our attitude and disposition. It can change our home and marriage. It has the power to change our relationships with others, and it certainly has the power to determine our eternal destiny.

Love is the essence of God, for "God is love."

> "In this is love, not that we have loved God but that he loved us and sent his Son to be the propitiation for our sins. Beloved, if God so loved us, we also ought to love one another. No one has ever seen God; if we love one another, God abides in us and his love is perfected in us" (1 John 4:10-12).

This is the essence of the gospel message, that God loves us and has prepared a way for us to be forgiven of our sins and brought back to a saving relationship with Him. From beginning to end the Bible is God's love letter to each one of us, detailing on every page God's love, concern, and willingness to forgive us. For those of us who are Christians, even while we were lost in sin God loved us (Romans 5:8). He loved us even when we refused to love Him (Romans 5:10), and it was God's great love for us that nailed Jesus to a cross and by grace and mercy obtained for us salvation. There certainly should never be anything that separates us from the love of God.

> "For I am sure that neither death nor life, nor angels nor rulers, nor things present nor things to come, nor powers, nor height nor depth, nor anything else in all creation, will be able to separate us from the love of God in Christ Jesus our Lord" (Romans 8:38, 39).

We should love God first and foremost. It is the greatest of all commandments.

> "And he said to him, 'You shall love the Lord your God with all your heart and with all your soul and with all your mind. This is the great and first commandment'" (Matthew 22:37,38).

Once we have mastered the love for God, then the second commandment becomes possible—to love our neighbors as we love ourselves. Yet everywhere we look, we can see sad evidences of the lack of love for God and for one another. So many people use His name in vain, cursing Him, when all He has ever done for us is good. The squandering of the opportunities with which He has blessed us and the lack of appreciation for these blessings, the evidence for the lack of love for God is seen as the masses of the world live for self and for personal gratification and pleasure. It is only when we recognize the incredible love of God that we have the possibility of conversion and change. Once we have come to a complete realization of what the love of God for us means, only then can we realize our true purpose for living—to please God and help one another.

There is proof that we do love God. We are commanded to "love one another…

> A new commandment I give to you, that you love one another: just as I have loved you, you are also to love one another. By this all people will know that you are my disciples, if you have love for one another" (John 13:34,35).

We are to love the brethren, our brothers and sisters (1 John 3:14). The lack of love for others is an indication of our lack of true love for God. We are to love God, to love our neighbors, to love our enemies, and to love the lost. It is that love for those people in our world who are blinded by sin that motivates us to evangelism and to the mission of Jesus—to seek and save the lost.

John's View of Love

I have always thought it interesting that there are millions of individual copies of the Book of John, primarily, I believe, because of his emphasis on love. New converts are often advised to read the Gospel of John, even before reading Matthew, Mark, or Luke. Certainly the tone of the book and the way he reveals the love of

CHAPTER 11

God and God's prophetic plan to save us is encouraging. John was first introduced to Jesus while he was a young man. Jesus came to the seashore and called James and his brother, John. They were fishing (Matthew 4:21).

James and John could not resist the call of the Lord. They traveled with Him day and night, listening to Him, observing His actions and manner of life, and witnessing the spirit of love that motivated everything He did. They saw His love and concern for the woman at the well, for the woman taken in adultery, and for the masses of people wandering as lost sheep, having no purpose. In watching Jesus, John saw God's love in action. John was privileged to stand beneath the cross as Jesus was crucified and witness firsthand God's love in its greatest sacrificial act. He came to understand that "God so loved the world, that He gave His only Son" to go from a humble manger at birth to a rugged cross at death.

As we grow older, the love of God should become more meaningful and our appreciation for all that God has done for us should become more inspiring. It is God's love that has sustained us through our Christian walk. God's love will see us in the transition from here to eternity. Even as we age, we should be sharing the love of God with others, letting people know of the mercy and grace of God that has been shown to us over and over again in our lives, testifying to the goodness of God and His saving power as we have experienced it in our lives.

In 1 John 4:10, 11, John describes the circular nature of God's love. First, he saw that he was a privileged recipient of God's love, and then he taught others to believe in God, to experience His love, and to pass that love on to one another. He also refused to let the world become the object of his primary love. The world and the things of the world often lead us in a wrong direction, away from God. John showed us the tight circle of love—God loved us first, therefore we ought to love one another, even our enemies, and then the circle goes back to God in that we love Him first and foremost. Yes, love carries a responsibility with it. Because God loves us, we have the responsibility of loving one another. One of the major qualities of love is that it goes beyond words. It is easy to say we love someone. It's more difficult to demonstrate that love by the way we live. It's easy to say we love God, but much more difficult to show that love by doing the will of God. The best definition of *love* is a visual one seen in the life of a true Christian as she serves, teaches, gives, and demonstrates the love of God both by her words and her actions. We need to thank God every day for the love He shows to us. We can't even imagine how meaningless our life would be without God's love and the provision of salvation and providential care that He offers to each one of us.

> "Then our mouth was filled with laughter, and our tongue with shouts of joy; then they said among the nations, 'The Lord has done great things for them'" (Psalm 126:2).

Growing Older in the Love and Grace of God

A test of true love is referenced in 1 Thessalonians 4:9.

> "Now concerning brotherly love you have no need for anyone to write to you, for you yourselves have been taught by God to love one another."

From the beginning of the church of Jesus Christ one of the litmus tests for genuine love and faith has been that Christians love one another. It is one of the acid tests that prove we love God. Certainly there are other proofs of our love for God, such as doing His will, keeping His commandments, accepting His plan of salvation, giving as we have been prospered, faithfully praying without ceasing, and worshiping regularly with God's people. But how we feel about and the way we treat one another as well as the motive for our relationships with one another, which must be love, is said to be a true indication of our love for God.

CHAPTER 11

We must never feel we are better than one of our brothers or sisters, that our education, financial considerations, or any other superficial circumstance or quality makes us better than anyone else. Our love is to be demonstrated in humility toward others. Remember the story in John 13. Jesus was about to face the greatest test of His life, and the most significant demonstration of His and God's love for us. He was literally standing in the shadow of the cross. But His thoughts were for His disciples, even though His betrayer had already set in motion the circumstances of His death. With the weight of the cross on His heart, Jesus said to His disciples,

> "A new commandment I give to you, that you love one another: just as I have loved you, you also are to love one another. By this all people will know that you are my disciples, if you have love for one another" (John 13:34,35).

Given the circumstances, this is an incredible insight to the depth of God's love demonstrated through Jesus Christ. Facing a cruel death and betrayed by one of His own disciples, instead of feeling sorry for Himself, Jesus was thinking about His disciples and teaching them again the true meaning of the word *love*.

How do we show true love for one another and our love for God? There are all kinds of physical, tangible objects that are meant to show who we are and how we feel about one another. There are the beautiful crosses we wear on necklaces and bracelets. There are many bumper stickers and emblems that are meant to show people who we are as Christians—the fish or "Honk if you love Jesus." I am certainly not criticizing these symbols of faith and commitment, but the best way to show people who we are and what we are about is to love one another. How are we showing the world that we love Jesus and that God is first in our lives? It is a question that each of us would do well to ask.

Author Francis Schaeffer says, "The mark that Jesus gives us to label a Christian, not just in one era or in one locality but at all times, all places, until Jesus returns, is the love we have for God and each other." He further states, "If Jesus turns to the world and says, 'I have something to say to you on the basis of my authority. I give you a right. You may judge whether or not an individual is a Christian on the basis of the love he shows to all Christians.'" Well, that's exactly what the Bible says. The proof of our love for God is demonstrated in our love for others. When Jesus washed the disciples' feet, He was teaching them how to love one another—demonstrating the valuable lesson of humility, showing them that in helping and sacrificing for one another, we are demonstrating the love of God. Read these verses... "Love one another with brotherly affection" (Romans 12:10); "And now I ask you...not as though I were writing you a new commandment, but the one we have had from the beginning—that we love one another" (2 John 5); "Let brotherly love continue" (Hebrews 13:1); "Above all, keep loving one another earnestly" (1 Peter 4:8); "Beloved, let us love one another, for love is from God, and whoever loves has been born of God and knows God. Anyone who does not love does not know God, because God is love. In this the love of God was made manifest among us, that God sent his only Son into the world, so that we might live through him. In this is love, not that we have loved God but that he loved us and sent his Son to be the propitiation for our sins. Beloved, if God so loved us, we also ought to love one another" (1 John 4:7-11); "And when he had taken the scroll, the four living creatures and the twenty-four elders fell down before the Lamb, each holding a harp, and golden bowls full of incense, which are the prayers of the saints" (Revelation 5:8); "You have kept count of my tossings; put my tears in your bottle. Are they not in your book?" (Psalm 56:8). Our prayers and tears are kept forever! Show your love; pray often.

I hope as we grow older in the love and grace of God, we will continue to realize and acknowledge the superiority of love and

CHAPTER 11

the necessity of demonstrating this love to one another, friends, family, brothers and sisters in Christ, even enemies, so that all of those around us will be attracted to Jesus because of the love they see demonstrated in our lives. Love covers a multitude of sins.

Questions

1. Discuss why love is one of the most written about and talked about topics among Christians.
2. What is the biblical definition of *love*?
3. How powerful is love?
4. In describing God, what is a three-word definition?
5. Discuss the first and second most important commandments.
6. Why is the Book of John so often recommended to be read first?
7. What is the circular nature of love?
8. What is a true test of love (1 Thessalonians 4:9)?
9. What are some ways we can show true love to one another and to God?
10. What is the proof of our love for God?
11. How does constant, fervent prayer keep us close to God and our love for Him and our fellow man alive?
12. What are some misconceptions about what love is?

CHAPTER 12

PREPARING TO DIE

A Little Wisdom

The content of one's character is not what he inherits from his ancestors, but what he leaves his descendants.

Decisions have descendants.

What we choose today, we live tomorrow.

"A good man leaves an inheritance to his children's children, but the sinner's wealth is laid up for the righteous" (Proverbs 13:22).

Actions can take you out of God's will but never out of His love.

"If we are faithless, he remains faithful—for he cannot deny himself" (2 Timothy 2:13).

A Little Humor

Perks of being 60 years old or more…

1. Kidnappers are not very interested in you.
2. In a hostage situation, you are likely to be released first.
3. No one expects you to run—anywhere.
4. People call at 8:00 p.m. and ask, "Did I wake you?"
5. People no longer view you as a hypochondriac.
6. There is nothing left to learn the hard way.
7. Things you buy now won't wear out.
8. You can eat supper at 4:00 p.m.
9. Your supply of brain cells is finally down to manageable size.

CHAPTER 12

Death Is not the End, but the Beginning

> "Whatever your hand finds to do, do it with your might, for there is no work or thought or knowledge or wisdom in [the grave], to which you are going" (Ecclesiastes 9:10).

We avoid the subject of death, not wanting to face our own or others' mortality. Death insurance is called "life insurance," and a graveyard is a "memorial garden." Hebrews 9:27 teaches us that, "It is appointed for man to die once...." Adam and Eve were never born, yet they died. Methuselah lived longer than anyone else in history, but he died. Samson was the strongest of all men. He, too, died. Moses was the meekest of men, yet he died. Solomon was said to have been the wisest man of his generation, but he died. Jesus never committed a sin, but He, too, died, that we might live eternally. Except for Elijah, Enoch, and perhaps Melchizedek, every one born of woman dies unless or until Jesus comes. Death is a certain fate. Isaiah 53:5,6:

> "But he was pierced for our transgression; he was crushed for our iniquities; upon him was the chastisement that brought us peace, and with his wounds we are healed. All we like sheep have gone astray; we have turned—every one—to his own way; and the Lord has laid on him the iniquity of us all."

The resurrection of Jesus gives each of us hope of eternal life.

We make preparation for almost every stage of life, except many never prepare for the most important transition—that of death. In 2 Kings 20:1-7, we read:

> "In those days Hezekiah became sick and was at the point of death. And Isaiah the prophet the son of Amoz came to him and said to him, 'Thus says the Lord, "Set your house in order, for you shall die; you shall not recover."' Then Hezekiah turned his face to the wall and prayed to the Lord, saying, 'Now, O Lord, please remember how I have walked before you in faithfulness and with a whole heart, and have done what is good in your sight.' And Hezekiah wept bitterly. And before Isaiah had gone out of the middle court, the word of the Lord came to him:

'Turn back, and say to Hezekiah, the leader of my people, Thus says the Lord, the God of David your father: I have heard your prayer; I have seen your tears. Behold, I will heal you. On the third day you shall go up to the house of the Lord, and I will add fifteen years to your life. I will deliver you and this city out of the hand of the king of Assyria, and I will defend this city for my own sake and for my servant David's sake.' And Isaiah said, 'Bring a cake of figs. And let them take and lay it on the boil, that he may recover.'"

King Hezekiah is told to get his house in order because he is going to die. He is sick with some sort of boil or sore on his body. After being told of his impending death by Isaiah, and struck with the full realization that his time was at hand, Hezekiah prayed to God that He might allow him to live a little longer. As a result of his godly life, and the fact that he was seeking to serve God as king, God granted his wish, and gave him an additional 15 years of life.

Each of us needs to put our house and keep our house in order, not knowing when we may die. The older we get, the more we realize there is less life left than we've already lived. We need to prepare for death, getting our business affairs in order. Our family should be protected in the event of our untimely death. We don't want to leave our loved ones struggling with debt. When we get our business affairs in order, it gives us peace of mind, knowing that in this way we have prepared for the inevitable. But even more important than protecting our family financially is getting our spiritual affairs in order. We need to prepare for the certainty of death (Hebrews 9:27).

Amos 4:12b says, "Prepare to meet your God...." It is only when we prepare spiritually that we can fully enjoy life, knowing that when we pass, we will be with the Lord throughout eternity.

"I tell you this, brothers: flesh and blood cannot inherit the kingdom of God, nor does the perishable inherit the imperishable. Behold! I tell you a mystery. We shall not all sleep, but we shall all

CHAPTER 12

be changed, in a moment, in the twinkling of an eye, at the last trumpet. For the trumpet will sound, and the dead will be raised imperishable, and we shall be changed. For this perishable body must put on the imperishable, and this mortal body must put on immortality. When the perishable puts on the imperishable, and the mortal puts on immortality, then shall come to pass the saying that is written: 'Death is swallowed up in victory.' 'O death, where is your victory? O death, where is your sting?'" (1 Corinthians 15:50-55).

Being prepared to die gives us freedom to truly live.

"For me to live is Christ, and to die is gain. If I am to live in the flesh, that means fruitful labor for me. Yet which I shall choose I cannot tell. I am hard pressed between the two. My desire is to depart and be with Christ, for that is far better" (Philippians 1:21-23).

Being a faithful Christian takes the fear out of death and helps provide victorious living. Our most-needed preparation is the preparation for death.

Hezekiah was both a good man and a good king. He understood the value and power of prayer. When faced with a deadly disease or circumstance, it is perfectly acceptable to ask God to extend your life if you believe you have work yet to be done. If God should for one reason or another extend your life by curing your illness, you should use whatever days you have left to the glory of God and service to others. The powerful words spoken here in 2 Kings 20:5, 6 let us know without doubt that God sees all, hears all and, most of all, responds to our needs and requests. (1) He says, "I have heard your prayer." (2) "I have seen your tears." (3) "I will heal you." (4) "I will add fifteen years to your life."

Too may people believe Satan's lie, "You will not surely die" (Genesis 3:4). I fear most people live as if this were true. We accumulate wealth and possessions as if we will never have to leave them. We seek power, prestige, and pleasure as if these are the only goals of living. When the end comes, many people are totally unprepared for what lies ahead. Unfortunately, we cannot prepare for death just by getting more education. Wise men, knowledgeable men, die just like the fool. All of the education in the world cannot save us from death. The wisest who have ever lived have not been able to avoid the grave. Most will never know far in advance what will take their life. It will most likely be some disease or an unforeseen accident.

Our congregation prays for the sick regularly, and we pray in faith. We pray for correct treatment, we pray for their doctors and nurses to use wisdom, we pray for their families, and their healing.

As a country, we spend billions of dollars every year trying to find cures for mankind's most prominent disease killers.

United States/2015

$ 5.418 billion	cancer
$ 5.015 billion	brain disorders
$ 4.327 billion	cardiovascular/heart/blood disease
$ 3.005 billion	HIV/AIDS
$ 1.261 billion	lung disease
$19.026 billion	TOTAL

This is how much we spent in one year trying to find a cure for these five diseases. According to the American Medical Association, we now spend more than $95 billion on research for cures to all diseases. Within a few years, that figure will rise to more than $100 billion, just for research. And this is only in the U.S. Other nations are spending large amounts on treatment and research for cures. Mankind is constantly trying to find a cure for all the diseases that ravage our bodies and cause death. There are physicians who spend their entire lives working on a cure that, until the day of their death, has not been discovered.

Recently, one of our members, Ken Sweeney, delivered a beautiful communion message, pointing out that of all the diseases we face, the most deadly and permanent one is sin. Sin is what

CHAPTER 12

separates us from God. Sin is what eats away at our soul like a cancer. Sin is what will keep us from heaven. But some years ago, there was one Physician who saw disease in our world and did everything possible to develop a cure. This one particular disease is one that troubles all of us. The research and planning had been done over thousands of years. For the last three years of His life, He worked tirelessly day and night to secure this cure for the greatest of all diseases. The cure would not be as many of our cures today are—so expensive that many can never afford it. This cure would be free. Anyone could accept it, regardless of race, color, language, nationality, or any of the barriers that separate men. It is ironic that when some found out that He had a cure, they did everything possible to kill Him, not realizing that His death would ensure the cure would become a reality. They finally took Him to court, gave false testimony, and had Him put to death, thinking they had eliminated the cure. Actually, with their wicked actions, they had ensured it. So even though today the disease is still with us, and every human is plagued by it, so is the cure. The cure is the blood of Jesus, shed for our sins.

> "But if we walk in the light, as he is in the light, we have fellowship with one another, and the blood of Jesus his Son cleanses us from all sin" (1 John 1:7).

Jesus, the Great Physician, offers His cure to everyone who will accept it, and by faith obediently seek to serve Him. His death, burial, and resurrection were God's prescription—the cure for sin.

Ironically, there are billions today who still refuse to accept the cure. Imagine, freedom from the consequences of sin without cost, freely given from the Great Physician, who died providing the cure! The salvation Jesus provides says that Satan does not get the last word. Jesus came to restore what was lost because of our sins and transgressions. He came to seek and save the lost (Luke 19:10). He came to bring life to sinners doomed to die (John 11:25). In dying, being buried, and then resurrected, He actually conquered two kinds of death. He conquered spiritual death,

"...even when we were dead in our trespasses, made us alive together with Christ—by grace you have been saved—and raised us up with him and seated us with him in the heavenly places in Christ Jesus, so that in the coming ages he might show the immeasurable riches of his grace in kindness toward us in Christ Jesus. For by grace you have been saved through faith. And this is not of your own doing; it is the gift of God, not a result of works, so that no one may boast" (Ephesians 2:5-9).

He also conquered physical death (1 Corinthians 15:55-57). Heaven, the promise for God's faithful, says that death does not get the last word. Being born again by the water and Spirit changes the destination of one's soul. For those who are saved by the blood of Christ, death is gain (Philippians 1:21). To depart and be with Christ is far better than any other experience of life or death. Jesus has prepared salvation for us here, and at this very moment, He is preparing a place for us in heaven.

Preparing for the Final Trip Home

God has a way of preparing us for our final departure. This preparation may come over a relatively long period of time, where we realize by subtle hints that we simply can't take care of ourselves any longer. Our body and mind may be giving way, and more and more there is a desire to simply go home for our final rest. I recently spoke with one of the members of our church who told me that her 90+ year old father was disappointed every morning when he woke up. He is so ready to go that he wants to pass in his sleep. When he doesn't, there is some disappointment. That's what I mean when I say God prepares us for our final trip. The inevitable reality sinks in that we are not meant to live here forever, and that there is something better waiting for us than the pain, suffering, forgetfulness, and disappointment of this life. Most of us have known people who, over and over before their death, have said "I'm ready to go. I want to go on and die." This is the final realization of God's preparing us for our passing.

CHAPTER 12

Food For Thought

"For if we live, we live to the Lord, and if we die, we die to the Lord. So then, whether we live or whether we die, we are the Lord's" (Romans 14:8).

"Everyone then who hears these words of mine and does them will be like a wise man who built his house on the rock. And the rain fell, and the floods came, and the winds blew and beat on that house, but it did not fall, because it had been founded on the rock" (Matthew 7:24,25).

"Yes, we are of good courage, and we would rather be away from the body and at home with the Lord" (2 Corinthians 5:8).

"No, in all these things we are more than conquerors through him who loved us. For I am sure that neither death nor life, nor angels nor rulers, nor things present nor things to come, nor powers, nor height nor depth, nor anything else in all creation, will be able to separate us from the love of God in Christ Jesus our Lord." (Romans 8:37-39).

Questions

1. Why do you think we mask the reality of death using veiled references to describe it?
2. In the history of mankind, how many people have avoided dying? Who were they?
3. What is significant about the death of Jesus?
4. Discuss the reasons why Hezekiah was allowed additional years of life.
5. What are some ways we should put our house in order, realizing that we all will die?
6. How does being prepared to die give us the freedom to truly live?
7. What was Satan's lie to Eve as well as to us regarding death?
8. Why and how should we pray for the sick regularly?

9. Will we ever, this side of eternity, find a cure for all of man's diseases and disorders?
10. What is the most deadly and significant disease known to man?
11. What is the cure for that deadly disease?
12. Why do you suppose so many people refuse the free cure for this disease?
13. How does God prepare us for our final departure?

CHAPTER 13

GOING HOME – HEAVEN

A Little Humor

In heaven, there were two huge signs. The first read, *Men Who Did What Their Wives Told Them To Do*. The line of men under this sign stretched as far as the eye could see. The second sign stated, *Men Who Did What They Wanted To Do*. Only one man stood under that sign. Intrigued, St. Peter said to the lone man, "No one has ever stood under this sign. Tell me about yourself." The man shrugged and said, "Not much to say; my wife told me to stand here." (Oscar Nunez, actor)

How Beautiful Heaven Must Be

> Then I saw a new heaven and a new earth, for the first heaven and the first earth had passed away, and the sea was no more. And I saw the holy city, new Jerusalem, coming down out of heaven from God, prepared as a bride adorned for her husband. And I heard a loud voice from the throne saying, "Behold, the dwelling place of God is with man. He will dwell with them, and they will be his people, and God himself will be with them as their God. He will wipe away every tear from their eyes, and death shall be no more, neither shall there be mourning, nor crying, nor pain anymore, for the former things have passed away."
>
> And he who was seated on the throne said, "Behold, I am making all things new." Also he said, "Write this down, for these words are trustworthy and true." And he said to me, "It is done! I am the Alpha and the Omega, the beginning and the end. To the thirsty I will give from the spring of the water of life without payment. The one who conquers will have this heritage, and I will

CHAPTER 13

be his God and he will be my son. But as for the cowardly, the faithless, the detestable, as for murderers, the sexually immoral, sorcerers, idolaters, and all liars, their portion will be in that lake that burns with fire and sulfur, which is the second death."

And the one who spoke with me had a measuring rod of gold to measure the city and its gates and walls. The city lies foursquare, its length the same as its width. And he measured the city with his rod, 12,000 stadia. Its length and width are equal. He also measured its wall, 144 cubits by human measurement, which is also an angel's measurement. The wall was built of jasper, while the city was pure gold, like clear glass (Revelation 21:1-8, 15-18).

Heaven will be a place that is perfect in every way. It will be a home place, with all the rich and wonderful meaning of that word—*home*. God the Father will be in heaven (Psalm 111:4; Revelation 4:1-5, 16). Jesus will be there.

> "Let not your hearts be troubled. Believe in God; believe also in me. In my Father's house are many rooms. If it were not so, would I have told you that I go to prepare a place for you? And if I go and prepare a place for you, I will come again and will take you to myself, that where I am you may be also" (John 14:1-3).

Heaven will be a wonderful resting place (Hebrews 4:3-11; 11:13-16). Yes, it will be perfect in every way, more than fulfilling all of our expectations. It will be big enough for all of God's faithful children. Revelation indicates it may be 1500 miles square, and it will be built of the most beautiful material imaginable to humans. But even with the description given in Revelation, I do not believe it is sufficient, because of our finite minds, to describe just how beautiful heaven will be. Revelation 21:18 offers the following description: "The wall was built of jasper, while the city was pure gold, like clear glass." The foundation of that city will be jasper, sapphire, agate, emerald, onyx, carnelian, chrysolite, beryl, topaz, chrysoprase, jacinth, and amethyst. The city will be lighted by the presence and glory of God, through Jesus Christ who will be the power source and light source through the 12 foundations, being reflected and prismed by the jasper of the city. The gates will be giant pearls, the street transparent gold. Each of God's children will have their own mansion room in that beautiful place. There will be many glorious, wonderful, rich blessings to be experienced. We will be in the presence of God, a place of ultimate holiness and righteousness (Revelation 22:3,4). Heaven will need no upkeep at all—no crumbling or decay, no urban renewal, no need for new paint or carpet, no dusting or vacuuming. There are no slums in heaven (1 Peter 1:4). Not even eternity can in any way exhaust the wonder, beauty, and permanence of heaven (Ephesians 2:7). There can be no greater security than the security God provides for His children. In heaven there will be no need for elaborate security systems to protect us from harm; no need to worry about hurting others' feelings, taking advantage of others, or the atrocities that humans inflict on each other here on earth. All of that will be gone. There will be no more pain, sorrow, suffering, or tears. It will all have passed away. Perpetual happiness, peace, and purpose are the perfect ingredients of heaven.

Finishing Well

For those of us who are older, it is essential that we finish the race well. We should use the wisdom we have acquired through years of experience to recognize what is important and what is not in this life. We should get rid of the excess weight that ties us to sin and causes us to be earthbound. We should concentrate on the good in life, which all comes from God, and should deliberately avoid the evil that plagues our lives. The call to those of us who are older is, "GET READY!" Make your calling and election sure. The finish line is in sight, and our best effort is required as we approach it.

Alan Carr, in an article on heaven, offers relevant insights. He writes about how Revelation gives us beautiful descriptions of heaven. These descriptions give the most precious of all elements

CHAPTER 13

and minerals known to man. Truly if we could see a place like that now, it would no doubt be breathtaking and almost overwhelming. But the truth is, I don't believe we can ever imagine just how spectacular and beautiful heaven will be, nor can we fully understand or know what heaven will be like. Using the very best adjectives and most descriptive language we have is not enough to describe the nature or the beauty of that wonderful place called heaven. The God who created this world and everything in it, and all of the universes our telescopes can reach out and see, created heaven, and Jesus is still preparing a place for each of God's faithful. Different civilizations have had their own concepts of what eternity or paradise must be like. To the Native Americans it was a "happy hunting ground," where the game was so plentiful that you never had to worry about your next meal or all of the products such as clothing and shelter, which could be provided by this teeming hunting ground.

When I was younger, I would hope that the Lord would not come because I had too many plans, aspirations, and dreams. Selfishly, I did not want anything to interfere with those plans. I am sure it was a failure on my part to recognize just how happy and secure we will be in heaven. I don't know what will occupy all of our time, but I do know that whatever it is God has in mind for us to do all day every day forever will be completely fulfilling and satisfying. As I have grown older, I have come to realize that heaven will be the fulfillment of whatever we need to complete our happiness and purpose for eternity. Yes, there will be singing, praising, and praying, as there should be, giving glory and honor to God for all He has done for us. Beyond that, I am not sure what God has in mind, but I am completely confident that it will be pleasing in every way and that there will never be a moment of boredom or regret, and the complete definition of perfect peace, purpose, and happiness will be fully understood. The beautiful passage that describes our understanding and acceptance of the gospel is one of those few passages that I believe has a double meaning, the latter applying to just how beautiful heaven will be.

> "But, as it is written, 'What no eye has seen, nor ear heard, nor the heart of man imagined, what God has prepared for those who love him'" (1 Corinthians 2:9).

Have you ever had similar feelings about what heaven must be like and wondered if there would be enough things to do there that you really enjoy? Let me reassure you that God is the activity director of heaven and, without question, it will be everything we in our wildest imagination could conceive it to be. As the problems associated with growing older creep up on us, we become more and more ready for such a place as heaven. Our sicknesses and infirmities, aches and pains, forgetfulness and growing lack of enthusiasm for this earth and all of its problems make us appreciate heaven with all of its promises.

The older we get, the more preparation we need to be making for that transition. We need to free our lives from any attitudes of unforgiveness, bitterness, or resentment. We need to let go of all the wrongs done to us over our lifetime and leave judgment to God. We need to free ourselves from any unfulfilled expectations of what we may have felt we were destined to be and simply for the rest of our life, however long that may be, to be a child of God living every day as close to Him as possible and looking forward to going home.

Food for Thought

> "But as it is, they desire a better country, that is, a heavenly one" (Hebrews 11:16).

As Peter neared the end of his life, he gave this good advice for preparation for heaven.

> "For this very reason, make every effort to supplement your faith

CHAPTER 13

with virtue, and virtue with knowledge, and knowledge with self-control, and self-control with steadfastness, and steadfastness with godliness, and godliness with brotherly affection, and brotherly affection with love. For if these qualities are yours and are increasing, they keep you from being ineffective or unfruitful in the knowledge of our Lord Jesus Christ" (2 Peter 1:5-8).

"But our citizenship is in heaven, and from it we await a Savior, the Lord Jesus Christ, who will transform our lowly body to be like his glorious body, by the power that enables him even to subject all things to himself" (Philippians 3:20, 21).

"...to an inheritance that is imperishable, undefiled, and unfading, kept in heaven for you" (1 Peter 1:4).

"Behold! I tell you a mystery. We shall not all sleep, but we shall all be changed, in a moment, in the twinkling of an eye, at the last trumpet. For the trumpet will sound, and the dead will be raised imperishable, and we shall be changed." (1 Corinthians 15:51,52).

Heaven will be a place of beautiful music (Revelation 5:9), a place of praise (Revelation 7:9-12), a place of service (Revelation 7:13-15), a place of comfort (Revelation 7:16,17), a place of rest (Revelation 14:13), and a place of rejoicing (Revelation 19:7). There will be no sickness, sorrow, or death (Revelation 21:1-6). What we endure here cannot be compared with what we will receive there (1 Thessalonians 4:13-18).

Questions

1. Discuss Revelation 21:1-8, 15-18. Who will not be in heaven?
2. Do you think that, with our finite minds, we can fully understand the beauty of heaven?

3. What is the light source for heaven?
4. Discuss the eternal permanence of heaven. Will it ever need any improvements?
5. As senior Christians, does the thought of heaven mean more to you now than it did when you were younger?
6. Who is the architect of heaven?
7. Do you feel differently about the Lord coming soon as an older Christian than you did when younger?
8. What is the dual meaning of 1 Corinthians 2:9?
9. Are the problems that we suffer here on earth in any way comparable to the gift of going to heaven?
10. What are some positive things we can do right now to prepare for going to heaven?
11. What is your favorite passage concerning heaven?
12. What are some negative things that will not be in heaven (Revelation 21:4)?

BIBLIOGRAPHY

Agus, David, and Kristin Loberg. *A Short Guide to a Long Life.* New York: Simon & Schuster, 2014.

Campbell, Roger. Preach For a Year: 104 *Sermon Outlines.* Place of publication not identified: Eisenbrauns, 2010.

Draper, James T. *Preaching With Passion: Sermons From the Heart of the Southern Baptist Convention.* Nashville, TN: Broadman & Holman Publishers, 2004.

Getz, Gene A. *Samuel: A Lifetime Serving God.* Nashville, TN: Broadman & Holman Publishers, 1997.

Getz, Gene A. *The Measure of a Man.* Ventura, CA: Regal Books, 2004.

God's Little Instruction Book: Inspirational Wisdom on How to Live a Happy and Fulfilled Life. Tulsa, OK: Honor Books, 1993.

Graham, Billy. *Nearing Home: Thoughts on Life, Faith, and Finishing Well.* Nashville, TN: Thomas Nelson, 2011.

Green, Joey, and Alan Corcoran. *You Know You've Reached Middle Age If—.* Kansas City, MO: Andrews McMeel Pub., 1999.

Laurie, Greg. *As It Is In Heaven: How Eternity Brings Focus to What Really Matters.* Colorado Springs: NavPress, 2014.

Ludy, Eric. *God's Gift to Women.* Sisters, Or.: Multnomah Publishers, 2003.

O'Connor, Karen. *God Bless My Senior Moments.* Eugene, OR: Harvest House Publishers, 2014.

O'Connor, Karen. *My Favorite Senior Moments.* Eugene, OR: Harvest House Publishers, 2015.

Ockenga, Harold John. *Women Who Made Bible History.* Grand Rapids: Zondervan Pub. House, 1962.

Redpath, Alan. *The Making of a Man of God: Studies in the Life of David.* Westwood, NJ: Revell, 1962.

Simmons, Matty, ed. "Funny People's Favorite Jokes." *Reader's Digest*, November 2015, 72-79.

Strand, Robert. *Live Fully, Laugh Often— And Don't Forget to Let the Cats Out!* Mobile, AL: Evergreen Press, 2012.

Vaughn, Donald. *Anti-Aging: Secrets to Help You Slow Down the Aging Process.* Adams, MA: F&W Publications Inc., 2002.

Webster, Allen. *Grandparent-ing.* House to House/Heart to Heart Tracts: Jacksonville, AL.

Wiersbe, Warren W. *Be Satisfied.* Wheaton, IL: Victor Books, 1990.

www.ingramcontent.com/pod-product-compliance
Lightning Source LLC
Chambersburg PA
CBHW022110090426
42743CB00008B/791